SIGHTREADING
AT THE
KEYBOARD

SIGHTREADING AT THE KEYBOARD

ROBERT SPILLMAN

SCHIRMER BOOKS
A DIVISION OF MACMILLAN, INC.
NEW YORK

COLLIER MACMILLAN CANADA
TORONTO

MAXWELL MACMILLAN INTERNATIONAL
NEW YORK   OXFORD   SINGAPORE   SYDNEY

Schirmer Books
A Division of Macmillan, Inc.
866 Third Avenue, New York, N.Y. 10022

Collier Macmillan Canada, Inc.
1200 Eglinton Avenue East, Suite 200
Don Mills, Ontario M3C 3N1

Library of Congress Catalog Card Number: 90-39278

Printed in the United States of America

printing number
1   2   3   4   5   6   7   8   9   10

Library of Congress Cataloging-in-Publication Data

Spillman, Robert
   Sightreading at the keyboard.

   Includes bibliographical references.
   1. Sight-reading (Music)   2. Piano—Studies and
exercises. I. Title.
MT236.S8   1990   90-39278
ISBN 0-02-872381-3

This book is lovingly dedicated
to the memory of

Jan DeGaetani,

a beautiful singer and a beautiful friend

Contents

LIST OF MUSICAL EXAMPLES   ix

PREFACE   xiii

CHAPTER 1. Some Thoughts on How
            We Learn Music   1

CHAPTER 2. How We Read   7

CHAPTER 3. Exercises in Rhythmic
            Stability and Harmonic
            Analysis   18

CHAPTER 4. Topographical Exercises   27

CHAPTER 5. Counterpoint   36

CHAPTER 6. Improvisation   41

CHAPTER 7. Transposing   48

CHAPTER 8. Score Reading   57

CHAPTER 9. Advanced Rhythmic and
            Notational Problems   68

CONCLUSION   75

SUGGESTED MUSIC FOR FURTHER STUDY   79

MUSICAL EXAMPLES   89

BIBLIOGRAPHY   267

List of Musical Examples

1. Schumann, Robert — *Album für die Jugend*, Opus 68, No. 1: "Melodie"
2. Schumann, Robert — *Album für die Jugend*, Opus 68, No. 3: "Trällerliedchen"
3. Schumann, Robert — *Album für die Jugend*, Opus 68, No. 6: "Armes Waisenkind"
4. Schumann, Robert — *Album für die Jugend*, Opus 68, No. 5: "Stückchen"
5. Bach, Johann Sebastian — *Notenbüchlein für Anna Magdalena Bach*, Menuet
6. Bach, Johann Sebastian — *Notenbüchlein für Anna Magdalena Bach*, Polonaise
7. Bach, Johann Sebastian — *Notenbüchlein für Anna Magdalena Bach*, Marche
8. Bach, Johann Sebastian — Little Prelude in D Minor, BWV 926
9. Schumann, Robert — *Album für die Jugend*, Opus 68, No. 14: "Kleine Studie"
10. Schumann, Robert — *Album für die Jugend*, Opus 68, No. 35: "Mignon"
11. Bartók, Béla — *For Children*, Volume 3, No. 13: "Anička Mlynárova"
12. Bartók, Béla — *For Children*, Volume 3, No. 14: "Plowing Are Six Oxen"
13. Bach, Johann Sebastian — Little Prelude in E Minor, BWV 941
14. Bartók, Béla — *For Children*, Volume 3, No. 5: "The Peacock Flew," measures 1–40
15. Bach, Johann Sebastian — Fughetta in C Minor, BWV 961
16. Bartók, Béla — *For Children*, Volume 4, No. 32: "Bagpipe Tune"
17. Bartók, Béla — *For Children*, Volume 4, No. 42: "Mourning Song"
18. Chopin, Frédéric — Prelude in B Minor, Opus 28, No. 6
19. Mendelssohn, Felix — *Songs Without Words*, Opus 19, No. 2: "Regrets"
20. Schumann, Robert — *Albumblätter*, Opus 124, No. 4: "Waltz"
21. Schumann, Robert — *Albumblätter*, Opus 124, No. 6: "Little Lullaby"
22. Scriabin, Alexander — Prelude in E Major, Opus 11, No. 9
23. Scriabin, Alexander — Prelude in C-Sharp Minor, Opus 11, No. 10
24. Schubert, Franz — Children's March in G Major, D. 928
25. Schubert, Franz — Four Ländler, D. 814
26a,b. Froberger, Johann — Two Sarabandes
27a,b,c,d. Kirnberger, Johann — Four Small Pieces: Polonaise, Menuet, *La Lutine*, *La Gaillarde*
28a,b. Marpurg, Friedrich — Two Small Pieces: Menuet, *La Badine*
29a,b. Nichelmann, Christoph — Two Small Pieces: *La Gaillarde, La Tendre*
30. MacDowell, Edward — *Sea Pieces:* "Starlight"
31. Schuman, William — *Three-Score Set:* II
32. Grieg, Edvard — *Lyric Pieces*, Opus 57, No. 6: "Hjemve," measures 28–56
33. Grieg, Edvard — *Lyric Pieces*, Opus 71, No. 2: "Sommeraften"

34. Bloch, Ernest — *Poems of the Sea:* "Chanty"
35. Bach, Johann Sebastian — Partita in A minor, BWV 827: Allemande, measures 1–6
36. Bach, Johann Sebastian — Sonata in G Major for Viola da Gamba and Cembalo, BWV 1027: *Adagio,* measures 1–8
37. Britten, Benjamin — *The Turn of the Screw,* tone-row
38. Berg, Alban — *Lulu,* tone-row
39. Berg, Alban — Concerto for Violin and Orchestra, tone-row
40. Schoenberg, Arnold — Five Piano Pieces, Opus 23, tone-row
41. Welcher, Dan — Dance Variations, tone-row
42. Foster, Stephen — "Old Folks at Home"
43. Foster, Stephen — "Beautiful Dreamer"
44. Anonymous — "The Nightingale"
45. Anonymous — "Barb'ry Allan"
46. Foster, Stephen — "Come Where My Love Lies Dreaming"
47. Monteverdi, Claudio — "Cor mio"
48. Monteverdi, Claudio — "Cruda Amarilli," measures 1–35
49. Verdi, Giuseppe — *Aïda:* Act II, Scene 2, measures 475–487
50. Anonymous — "The Riddle Song"
51. Anonymous — "The Inconstant Lover"
52. Anonymous — "The Mingo Mountains"
53. Anonymous — "Go Bury Me Beneath the Willow"
54. Handel, Georg Friedrich — *Neun deutsche Arien:* No. 1, "Künft'ger Zeiten"
55. Bach, Johann Sebastian — Cantata *Gott, der Herr, ist Sonn' und Schild* (BWV 79): Aria, "Gott ist unser Sonn' und Schild!"
56. Bach, Johann Sebastian — Cantata *Gott, der Herr, ist Sonn' und Schild* (BWV 79): Chorale, "Nun danket Alle Gott"
57. Bach, Johann Sebastian — Cantata *Gott, der Herr, ist Sonn' und Schild* (BWV 79): Chorale, "Erhalt' uns in der Wahrheit"
58. Bach, Johann Sebastian — Cantata *O Ewigkeit, du Donnerwort* (BWV 60): Chorale, "Es ist genug"`
59. Bach, Johann Sebastian — Cantata *Sie werden aus Saba Alle kommen* (BWV 65): Chorale, "Ei nun, mein Gott"
60. Mozart, Wolfgang Amadeus — Divertimento, K. 113: *Allegro,* measures 1–53
61. Mozart, Wolfgang Amadeus — Divertimento, K. 131: Menuet
62. Mozart, Wolfgang Amadeus — Divertimento, K. 186: *Allegro assai;* Menuet
63. Beethoven, Ludwig van — Symphony No. 7 in A Major, Opus 92: I: *Poco sostenuto; vivace,* measures 63–94
64a. Mendelssohn, Felix — *Ein Sommernachtstraum:* III. Song with Chorus, measures 1–8
64b. Mendelssohn, Felix — *Ein Sommernachtstraum:* III. Song with Chorus, measures 44–59
65. Wagner, Richard — *Lohengrin,* Act III: measures 1–48
66. Haydn, Franz Joseph — Quartet in B-flat Major, Opus 64, No. 2: Menuetto
67. Mozart, Wolfgang Amadeus — Quartet in G Major, K. 156: *Presto*
68. Mozart, Wolfgang Amadeus — Quintet in B-flat Major, K. 174: *Menuetto ma allegretto*

69. Schumann, Robert — "So lasst mich scheinen," Opus 98a, No. 9: measures 1–19

70. Schumann, Robert — "Zigeunerliedchen," Opus 70, No. 8

71. MacDowell, Edward — Second Concerto for Piano and Orchestra in D Minor, Opus 23: III, measures 126–144

72. Gluck, Christoph Willibald von — *Orfeo ed Euridice:* "Che puro ciel"

73. Mahler, Gustav — "Liebst du um Schönheit"

74. Holst, Gustav — *Sāvitri,* measures 177–199

75. Ravel, Maurice — *Ma Mère l'Oye:* II. "Petit Poucet"

76. Ravel, Maurice — *L'Enfant et les Sortilèges,* measures 1–40

77. Murgier, Jacques — Capriccio for Oboe and Piano

78. Reynolds, Verne — Echo Variations for Oboe and Piano: III. "Crystals"

79. Hindemith, Paul — Sonata for Viola and Piano, Opus 11, No. 4: II. Theme and Variations, measures 1–33

80. Hindemith, Paul — Sonata for Violoncello and Piano Opus 11, No. 3: II, measures 82–109

81. Harris, Roy — *Little Suite:* I. "Bells"

82. Satie, Erik — *Gnossienne,* No. 1

83. Satie, Erik — *Descriptions Automatiques:* I. "Sur un Vaisseau"

84. Satie, Erik — *Airs à faire fuir:* III

85a. Martinů, Bohuslav — Trio: III. *Allegro,* measures 1–9

85b. Martinů, Bohuslav — Trio: III. *Allegro,* measures 21–31

85c. Martinů, Bohuslav — Trio: V. *Allegro con brio,* measures 50–80

86. Puccini, Giacomo — *Madama Butterfly,* Act I, measures 1–31

87a. Welcher, Dan — *Dance Variations:* Variation I, measures 9–30

87b. Welcher, Dan — *Dance Variations:* Variation VI, measures 28–34

88a. Reynolds, Verne — Quintet for Piano and Winds: I. Toccata, measures 1–7

88b. Reynolds, Verne — Quintet for Piano and Winds: II. Cantilena, measures 1–14

88c. Reynolds, Verne — Quintet for Piano and Winds: III. *Allegro,* measures 36–46

89a. Schoenberg, Arnold — *Pierrot Lunaire,* "Mondfleck," measures 13–16

89b. Schoenberg, Arnold — *Pierrot Lunaire,* "Die Kreuze," measures 5–9

90. Schumann, Robert — *Allegro in B Minor,* Opus 8, measures 105–139

91. Xenakis, Iannis — *Herma,* measures 89–113

92. Stockhausen, Karlheinz — *Klavierstück IX,* measures 134–152

93. Bedford, David — *Piano Piece 2,* lines 1–5

94. Feldman, Morton — *Durations III* for Violin, Piano, and Tuba: II

95. Brown, Earle — *Music for Cello and Piano,* lines 1–3

96. Steffen, Wolfgang — *Les Spirales,* Opus 36, lines 1–5

97. Albright, William — Five Chromatic Dances: III. Fantasy—Mazurka, lines 1–3

98a. Ince, Kamran — *Beyond Black,* lines 1–6

98b. Ince, Kamran — *Beyond Black,* lines 38–43

Preface

When I speak to groups of musicians, whether they are students, teachers, or amateurs, I frequently come around to a favorite topic of mine, the importance of sightreading skills in professional musical careers. I will discourse enthusiastically on audition situations in which people have had to sightread in front of a potential employer and on the opportunities that opened up because of them. I will encourage everyone in the group to learn to sightread or to practice in order to sightread better. Often, after I have warmed to the subject, someone will stop me, voice heavy with disbelief, to ask, "Can you really *learn* to sightread?" The implication is that some people are born with great sightreading ability; there is no method involved. It is often implied, if there is further discussion, that people get better only by reading large amounts of music and that people without some sort of innate talent will never get better, no matter how hard they try.

The question might therefore be better stated, Can sightreading be taught? Obviously, since I am writing this book, my answer is yes; and I hope that the drills, exercises, and discussions in this book will prove to be helpful to musicians at all levels of advancement.

This book is designed mainly for use in college-level classrooms. Although individuals could practice the exercises at home, and friends could get together without a teacher, I will shape my discussions with a teacher-student setup in mind. This does not mean, however, that I consider the book to be useless in self-help situations. For those students who are working alone, I have tried to make the discussions and explanations clear and complete.

A good arrangement for a sightreading class is a group of four students meeting with a teacher in a room where there are two pianos. A teacher can, of course, handle larger groups, but the effectiveness of the hands-on experience is diminished by having too many people share the time. A teacher can also teach reading one-on-one, but this quickly deteriorates into practicing with the student and is likely to be a waste of the teacher's time. Three students in a group constitute a dangerous number psychologically; four seems both congenial and manageable.

Four pianists at two pianos might not be a grouping encountered frequently today, but it was an arrangement that was quite popular among musicians in the latter part of the nineteenth century. Musicians such as Saint-Saëns and Fauré became acquainted with the latest masterworks through such arrangements; disciples of Wagner rushed to publish versions of his works for piano solo, piano four-hands, two pianos, *and* two pianos, eight hands. Before the advent of the phonograph, the parlor piano was the normal means of learning about the state of music, and many parlors had more than one instrument. I have listed a sampling of the eight-hand music you could find in print around 1900 on pages 84–87; alas, most of these treasures are out of print today, found only in libraries and old storerooms. There are a few items still published (the Handel, Grainger, and some of the Brahms dances), but nothing like the abundance to be found in the days before the rise of the long-playing record and the tyranny of the profit margin.[1]

It will be evident to the thoughtful teacher or student that it would be impossible for me to collect all the music necessary for a course in sightreading into one volume. There is simply not enough room in one book for enough music to feed the appetites of a group of students who are constantly devouring new material. It is also evident that some of this new material should not be in a book that will be readily available to the students if it is to be read *prima vista*; if it is sightreading, then it has to be at least partially surprising.

On pages 79–87 I have compiled a list of suggestions for additional material. Such a list is doomed to be not only very personal and idiosyncratic but also severely limited in scope. I have listed music that has worked for me in studying sightreading, but each teacher and student can easily assemble a goodly selection, either from a library or from a private collection.

---

[1] You might wonder why I am spending time talking about eight-hand arrangements. One reason is that ensemble playing is a very important part of learning to play and read well. We pianists spend too much time alone at our instrument, compared to singers and orchestral musicians, and so rob ourselves of the pleasure and challenge of keeping time with others. The more you can find an opportunity to play with someone else, whether singer, instrumentalist, or fellow keyboard player, the more dependable and assured your rhythm will be. Rhythm is the basis on which we can build our music, and rhythmic dependability is one of the most basic skills we need in order to become good sightreaders.

SIGHTREADING
AT THE
KEYBOARD

Chapter 1

SOME THOUGHTS ON HOW WE LEARN MUSIC

This book is addressed to those musicians who feel that they would like to do more in the world of music—to play more and to use their musical abilities more frequently. Often a child studying music is asked by his elders, "What are you going to *do* with your music?" I am assuming that you, the reader, want to "*do* something with your music," that you want to be asked to play, and that you want to play well, perhaps even professionally. You have practiced for years, and you wish to keep improving. You wish to be useful and, to use a crass word, marketable.

In order to enter the world of supply and demand as a keyboard player, there are several avenues open to you. You can become a member of a band, be it rock, jazz, or polka, by learning to control the proper instruments and appropriate styles. You can learn to play hymns and accompany the choir and congregation by learning that particular repertoire and style. You can play for dance classes, if your sense of rhythm and your imagination are good enough. You can find occasions on which to play solos or duos or to accompany colleagues on the flute or violin, or in songs. You can work to enter the world of concerts or of opera as a coach or colleague, by learning the proper repertoire. On your way to fulfillment of these goals, you may have to do all sorts of journeyman labor, playing the organ in church or playing the piano for variety shows, funerals, cocktail lounges, and school assemblies. I am not belittling any form of work you may be able to do with your hands; I have done all of the things I have mentioned, and more. The skills needed for all of these jobs are interrelated; playing in church or playing onstage, you will always require accuracy, style, and musical intelligence.

One truth should be emphasized, moreover; in the world of music, one of the most basic, essential, sought-out, and appreciated of these musical skills is the ability to sightread. A working pianist must be able to absorb and reproduce music at once. If one can do this, he or she will get the better classes, the better church jobs, the better shows, and also, with luck and application, the songs and sonatas one may aspire to. Every working pianist I know got to be a member of the professional ranks either by winning big on the competition circuit (which takes both dedication and a good amount of luck) or by sightreading very, very well.

We are likely to say "She's a good sightreader" in the same way we would say "She has blue eyes," implying that the ability to read music *prima vista* is an innate talent, an athletic ability that is bestowed divinely on certain fortunate individuals. Indeed, different people have differing levels of skill; some people have more inhibitions than others, some are nearsighted, some even dyslexic. It is my firm belief, however, that focusing on this disparity of skill is evading the issue. Some people are better at balancing their checkbook than others, but we all have to give it a try, at least.

Another mistake heard in discussions of the music profession is the categorizing of various skills. One often hears mention of a great gap between those who sightread and those who "play by ear." It is often thought that the two skills are mutually exclusive, with the result that someone who improvises well never works on sightreading, and vice versa. This is tragic, as the two skills are interrelated and can be cultivated simultaneously.

A pertinent point to consider is this: it is very difficult to be a working musician on any level if you cannot read and absorb music quickly and efficiently. The person who can read through the score of a musical comedy with little trouble will be asked to play for the production, while the person who has to memorize the entire book before the first rehearsal will not. The pianist who can read songs or sonatas will be asked to come around for an evening of chamber music, in preference over the one who has only one piece memorized and ready. The pianist who can sightread will get the jobs, whether in a school, a church, or on the concert stage. It is not a matter of natural or divine dispensation whether you can read or not; it is a matter of survival.

Let me give you some examples. Pianist A knocks on the door of a famous string player's studio and asks for work. The famous string player hands her the manuscript score of a new concerto and says, "I'm free in two hours. Come back then and rehearse this with me." Pianist B goes to accompany a friend's lesson with a famous voice teacher. The famous voice teacher says, "Take this down a step. It sounds too high in her voice." Musician C studies conducting for years and applies for a job as assistant conductor in an opera house. For his audition he is asked to play the opening of *Porgy and Bess*, the voice parts only of the Council Scene from *Otello*, the first-act finale from *Don Giovanni*, and the opening of *Der junge Lord*.

Once A impresses the famous teacher and gets her job, she may play for twenty cello students at their weekly lessons, covering a lot of sonatas and concertos. She might play a different cello recital every few weeks or might go on tour, playing such works as the Britten or Dohnányi sonatas a dozen times in a dozen cities. After B starts working for the famous voice teacher, he may find himself playing thirty opera and oratorio arias a day in lessons, or reading through the piano parts of a famous diva's operatic role, or teaching the notes of a piece to a slow learner. If C lands that job in the opera house, he will find himself playing for rehearsals of a dozen different operas, sitting at the piano in a roomful of people where he and a conductor are the two people who are supposed to know what's really going on with the music.

These stories are not only typical, they are taken from real life, with only a slight amount of amalgamation on my part. A, B, and C are recognizable as specialists in instrumental accompanying, vocal accompanying, and opera coaching, respectively. Very few of us get to specialize in one of these areas exclusively, however; more often we are called upon to leap from one repertoire to another at a moment's notice. What is important and unifying in these examples is that the people are working as musicians and that they got their jobs because they could sightread.

If they are to keep working, they will not only have to sightread, they will also have to develop related skills as well. Pianist A might have to perform a baroque sonata that is in manuscript, where there is nothing on the page but the solo line and a figured bass—and, to add to her problems, the two voices may not line up with each other on the page. Accompanist B may have to try a few songs by Mahler or Strauss in several different keys, transposing at sight, until a singer can decide in which key her voice is the most comfortable. Musician C may find that the job of teaching a singer all of his role involves being able to sing all the other parts in order to give cues.

Let us take some time to examine more closely some of the aspects of learning as they apply not only to A, B, and C but also to you and me.

THRESHOLDS OF LEARNING

When learning a piece of music, we have all had experiences that are akin to arriving at different levels. Sometimes we reach a plateau; nothing seems to be improving despite constant, faithful effort on our part. On Wednesday we cannot get a passage to be fluent, no matter how assiduously we try. Then, miraculously, we find that the same passage flows effortlessly the first time we play it on Thursday. These sudden shifts can be called thresholds; these are times when we notice that we have somehow solved some difficulty and left it behind us.

Some music is simple enough that we can play it through once and feel as though we possess it. Often a piece will fall into this category except for one or two spots where we must pay extra attention. It is especially interesting to examine the reasons for those difficulties. Some of the common causes are:

· increased technical difficulty
· musical language beyond our normal vocabulary
· awkward layout on the page
· counterproductive fingering
· wrong notes read the first time
· increased rhythmic complexity
· register shifts.

At the other end of the spectrum we find music that remains opaque and intransigent until we memorize it. In cases like this there is no "threshold" of comfort to be found anywhere in the learning process; while we are still reading, we are living on the edge, exercising mental control, naming everything as it appears, defining shapes as they pass before our eyes, and hoping that we can include all of the features in any given measure. There are usually passages that remain stubbornly foreign to us and that we will have to check every time we play. The causes of these difficulties are, however, the same as those on the list above. After we pass over a threshold called memorization, these problem spots become places where a conscious effort is required to remember, to label, and to find the notes or hand positions. If we perform a memorized piece many times, these problem places may eventually become almost as automatic and comfortable as the easier stretches, with our minds registering only a flicker of awareness that something unusual is passing by.

Let us go back for a moment to one of our examples, Pianist B, and examine what sort of reading he will find himself doing in his working situation. He might go to accompany a voice lesson not knowing what he will have to play that particular day. First, the soprano whose lesson it is pulls out "Caro nome" from Verdi's *Rigoletto*, which he has played two dozen times. He will be a stage closer to memorization than to *prima vista* reading, mostly playing by ear as his eyes graze over the page, noticing the E chord in the strange position or noting the approach of the troublesome sixths. Next the singer sets "Ah, non credea" from Bellini's *La Sonnambula* in front of him, an aria that he has played only once. Now he will be reading more "purely," taking the patterns from the page before him and organizing them almost instantaneously. His task will be easy on two levels: musically the harmonies and figures are quite simple to someone who has heard a lot of music, and technically the figures are easy and slow-paced. B will probably have an easier, more relaxing time than with "Caro nome," because that aria was more demanding technically even though he almost knew it by heart.

An important point to notice is that the difficulties one has in reading fall into three large categories:

· the musical language is obscure
· the technical requirements are high
· the layout on the page is unclear.

The third type of problem, that of layout, is eliminated after a few readings of any composition; the jumps from line to line or from page to page, the extreme ledger lines, the awkward arrangements of notes—all must be sorted out early in the learning process in order for the playing to become fluent. The first two groups of problems, however, remain to a varying degree in every stage of learning. A new piece may have, for example, more technical complexities than musical ones. The first few readings will therefore be hesitant for the sake of our fingers, even after our ears may already know what to expect. These technically difficult places will eventually become as fluent as the easier parts of the composition, but in the sequence that goes from fluency to memorization will require a little extra effort each time we come to them. Finally, after memorization, these will be the passages where we will have to pay special attention technically in order to perform the entire work well. The same is, of course, true for passages that offer musical problems; long after memorization, these places will cause us to wake up and concentrate.

Let us return to pianist B one last time. Perhaps the teacher brings out Anne Trulove's aria from Stravinsky's *The Rake's Progress*. Now B is in trouble; he has never seen this music before. He has heard it perhaps once or twice and considers it to be amazingly difficult. Now he remains on the first threshold, having to count consciously at all times, to listen, to analyze harmonies, to recognize and reproduce chord formations, and to phrase shapes instantaneously.

It is probable that his worst problem in reading this third aria will be one of controlling his panic. It is true that the music is frequently complex in its language and that the technical difficulties are formidable; but it is also true that terror or self-recrimination are not useful tools in solving the problem of how to play any passage. A scenario such as I have described happens many times every day in the music world, and it is neither unfair nor unrealistic to assume that there will be pianists who can rise to the challenges set before them.

In the particular case of pianist B and the Stravinsky aria, his raw materials will still be the same as in the simpler arias that preceded it. Some of these, for example, are

1. 6/8 time—the number of eighth notes and sixteenth notes in a bar, and the normal arrangement of dotted quarters.
2. 4/4 time—the number of halves, quarters, eighths, sixteenths, and combinations thereof in a bar, the normal method of barring sixteenth notes, and the sense of a 4/4 pulse at a certain speed.
3. B minor—the tones in the tonic, the tones that are embellishing or nonharmonic, the notes in the dominant chord, and the tones in the various forms of the scale.
4. C major—the same norms of reference.
5. basic rhythmic patterns, such as the relative speed of eighths and quarters in the same passage.
6. basic contour facts, such as the shape of a diatonic scale on the page and under the hand.

As you can see, pianist B has a large number of facts ready to help him as he starts to read. To see how some of these actually translate into action, it is necessary to examine more closely how we read anything, including words.

Chapter 2

HOW WE READ

I want to go to the seashore.

If you could have observed your actions and reactions as you read through the sentence above, you would have seen[1] that your eyes took in a group of words—in this case most probably the first four—in one glance. Then your eyes involuntarily leaped to the next group of words and focused on them. You did not read one word at a time. All of the words at the beginning of the sentence were almost instantaneously recognized to be familiar, simple, and arranged according to grammatical rules that you have learned and used; and so you grouped the words together.

Furthermore, your conscious mind was already in an act of interpretation, looking forward, through a time span that was most probably approximately one-fifth of a second, to discovering exactly *where* it was that you wanted to go. The only part of this sentence that required you to spend any more than a small fraction of a second focusing on it could have been the final word; first, because it is suddenly longer than every word that preceded it; second, because it contains some interesting—that is, unusual—letter combinations (*seas*, for example, which we know as an independent unit but which seems to be the wrong word division in the present usage); and, third, precisely because your brain has comprehended the incipient meaning of the sentence, even before it has been completed, and is waiting to find out what the object of desire is—*where* do I want to go?

The involuntary leaps that the eyes manage, called saccades, normally take only one-fiftieth of a second, while the focusing that occurs afterward takes up to one-twentieth of a second. The brain seems to handle the control of these movements with no help from our conscious will, arriving at the place where we need to look with amazing accuracy considering the speed; indeed, the only eye movement that we can control at will is a moderately slow sweep in one direction. Another interesting aspect of the speed of eye movements is that hand movements fall into the same sort of time span: we can move our hands to a "place of focus" in about one-twentieth of a second. Furthermore, larger leaps of both eyes and hands are done

---

[1] This is assuming, of course, that you are not in the first grade and just learning to read, and that English is your mother tongue.

through more rapid movement than are shorter leaps. There is much scientific evidence that eye-hand coordination is not only natural but also amazingly efficient and well-developed in human beings. The short-term memory of our brain, however, erases all information after a very short span: on average, after one-fifth of a second all information passed to the brain is either consolidated into some larger conglomeration of features and details called a schema or is forgotten.

If you are like the overwhelming majority of English-speaking people, you read our sample sentence without "hearing" it in your inner ear. The capability of hearing it is there, latent in your mind, as is the capability of looking away from the page and "seeing" it before your inner eye. Let us assume, however, that you are a radio or television announcer who is to read our sample sentence on the air. If we have a scenario in which you are handed a bulletin containing the sentence while you are on the air, you will speak it aloud the first time you see it, and the rate at which your eyes proceed will be somewhat restrained by the kinetic action (the motion of your mouth) that is involved. Nevertheless, the pace at which most of us can read this sentence aloud is rapid; you will probably finish it within a second, unless you are trying for a more distinct, "elocutionary" effect. Our speed in reading this sentence is thus reduced from around two-fifths of a second when silent to around four-fifths of a second when spoken; the number of saccades, however, is probably still only two.

Most radio and television speakers are in the habit of reading something through silently before they have to speak it, and they try to get their hands on their material early enough so that this can be possible. This action produces an interesting and somewhat different constellation of brain activities. The eye motions will be the same as for silent reading, but the brain will also ask for what is, in effect, a sound track and will listen to the sound of the spoken language (which is not at all a direct equivalent to the written language) as the words are read. We have all, since the first grade, become accustomed to the time delay that is involved in reading; a fluent reader's eyes are focused approximately five words in front of what his brain is assimilating. In the case of the studying radio or television announcer, there is also an interesting time lapse; what his brain "hears" or, more accurately, creates in sound, runs at the speed of his/her speech, while what the brain "sees" or, more accurately, assembles, has been received about twice as fast.

At the same time, the reader can formulate some judgments. For example, even in a statement as simple as "I want to go to the seashore" there is an automatic judgment that our brains can accomplish that establishes the hierarchy of the words; unless the announcer has had time to rehearse—that is, to test various possibilities—he or she will lump "Iwant" and "togo" together, slip through "tothe" quickly without stress, and designate "seashore" as the focal point of the sentence, that word or phrase which distinguishes this sentence from all other "I want to go to the . . ." sentences. The announcer might also realize that the word "seashore" could demand a bit of practice, either because its aspect on the page is slightly unusual or because the announcer associates it with a tongue twister ("She sells seashells by the seashore") learned and kept as part of previous experience. In other words, we read through the vast majority of sentences by lumping as much as possible into patterns (schemata). One of the divisions we make naturally is between easy words like "I" and more complex words like "seashore"; also, the relative complexity of some words could be caused either by their newness and strangeness ("I want to go to the cenotaphs") or by a remembered piece of a puzzle ("seashore" is part of a tongue twister).

Now let us examine a sentence from a poem by Alfred Lord Tennyson that will allow us to discuss other facets of the process of reading.

Now sleeps the crimson petal, now the white;

As soon as we look at the shapes that comprise the first three words, we are likely to stop for a fraction of a second. Most people will backtrack, or make a saccade to the left. This is not because the words are unfamiliar; we have encompassed all three of them in our vocabularies since very early childhood, if we grew up speaking English. We pause because the grammar is momentarily puzzling: we are used to seeing (also hearing and speaking) the word "sleeps" after its subject, and so our brain searches for it, looking in vain for a noun or pronoun in the space after "Now." For most readers, the time it takes to leap backward, approximately one-fifth of a second, will suffice for the mind to formulate the explanation: there is inverted word order at work here, and we should expect a subject to appear at some future time.

After this simultaneously effected judgment on the part of our brain, we are free to leap forward and assimilate "the crimson petal." The word "crimson" in this sentence plays a similar role to "seashore" in our first one; it has a few ambiguous formulations, such as the total lack of ascending or descending lines in its letters, and it would deserve at least the fleeting attention of someone who was to read the sentence aloud. The final phrase, "now the white," has its own ambiguities; almost anyone reading this poem for the first time needs to backtrack from the semicolon to be assured that the subject ("petal") is missing and to supply it, the brain fleshing out the schema.

Thus the brain is continually molding together and making sense out of what the eyes relate to it. Indeed, scientists will speak of the brain telling the eyes what to see, rather than the reverse; our eyes are basically told to search for clues that will confirm or adjust what the brain needs to absorb the information being communicated through the act of reading. I played a little trick on you in similar fashion by announcing, before you saw the sentence in question, that it would be from a poem. This revelation on my part immediately alerted you to seek those attributes which you have, through many years' experience, learned to relate to "poemness." The inverted word order, therefore, stymied you only for, at the most, one-fifth of a second. In the case of a small child first learning to read, however, or someone first learning to read English, such an event in a line of words could cause a complete breakdown of forward motion until a suitable reason was forthcoming, either through consultation with an expert (parent, teacher, or other), or through a self-invented explanation.

Another effect of the announcement at the onset of "poemness," in most experienced readers, is an increase in attention paid to the sound of words and phrases; in other words, most of us automatically start to conjure up the sounds of the words we are reading, bridging the gap between spoken English and written English.[2]

The intelligent reader can see many parallels to music. For example, how many times teachers ask students who are about to read a new piece to "check the key and time signatures!" This sets up expectations in much the same way as my use of the word "poem" set up expectations in your reading of the Tennyson line. If we know what comprises E-flat major, our brains tell our eyes to search for familiar landmarks. If we are familiar with minuets as a category, we will expect three quarter-note beats, and the discovery of a measure that has only 2½ beats would stop us as surely as "Now sleeps" would stop a beginner at English.

Let us turn from prose and poetry and analyze briefly the process of reading a similarly short section of music, the opening of the last movement of Beethoven's Sonata in C Minor, Opus 13 (Exercise 2–1).

EXERCISE 2–1. LUDWIG VAN BEETHOVEN, SONATA PATHÉTIQUE IN C MINOR, OPUS 13, OPENING OF THE THIRD MOVEMENT

If you take a few moments to observe your mental processes while looking at this portion of the music, you will start to see how some of the actions are similar to those employed when reading words

---

[2] This gap is much wider than many people suspect; it is not as wide, of course, as Chinese or Japanese but much more complex and less likely to yield one-to-one formulations than, for example, Italian.

Figure 2–1. Probable eye-division of the passage from Beethoven's Sonata
in C Minor

Figure 2—2. Contour of the passage

Figure 2–3. Rhythm of the passage

Figure 2–4. Treble and bass clef in normal position

Figure 2–5. Incorrect rhythmic grouping in the Beethoven passage

and sentences, and how they differ. You might have, for example,
tried to fasten your eyes immediately on the treble line and observed not only the formulations of sounds in your so-called inner
ear but also the automatic twitching of the fingers of your right
hand as they sought out the proper muscular patterns. If you had
really succeeded in seeing only the notes of the treble part, with no
prior clues, your eyes would have jumped to the first four notes,
then the next two, and then the next two, as in Figure 2–1. You
could also hear the contour of the line, as demonstrated in Figure

2–2. Given a certain level of experience with musical notation, you could also feel or sense the rhythm, as in Figure 2–3.

Did you also feel a tension in your fingers which denotes their readiness to serve the brain? After a few years of playing an instrument, this kinesthetic response is present in a musician's nervous system, whether it is consciously asked for or not.

If you had been looking only at notes, you might have received a shock when you reached the second half of the second measure and encountered a natural sign in front of the B. If you had not previously known that the selection was in minor, your first choice would probably have been to play the first eight notes of the melody in C major. Upon assimilating the natural sign in measure 2, however, you would have done one of two things; either you would have performed a giant leap backward to observe the key signature, located far to the left of your present line of vision or, if you had assumed that the first eight notes were really in conformity with the requirements of C major and you were looking for that, you simply redirected your definitions and commanded your eyes to return to the brain clues that corresponded to the configuration "C minor." Obviously it is quicker and more efficient if you are so versed in the schemata of tonalities that you do not require the time-consuming leap to the left at this point. A somewhat parallel point could be made in the Tennyson line: if you had already assimilated the word inversion and the concept *crimson petal* by the time your eyes saw the grouping *now the white*, you could differentiate what was more important in the latter phrase and place it in a parallel position to *crimson* rather than creating an incorrect parallelism: *Now sleeps the = Now the white.*

There are, of course, many other "cultural" clues that are given to us at the beginning of the piece of music. From prior acculturization, that is, from the body of knowledge that you have learned so far, you can categorize *Rondo*. You will know to expect the first parcel of music to return at least twice before the movement ends. This bit of information may be set aside as being not very practical at the moment. For one thing, you are more interested in reading the first parcel correctly than in anticipating its return; for another, you may have already learned not to trust composers to be exact in their returns, having seen several examples where the return of a theme is altered or disguised. *Allegro* will be very useful, however, if it is noted. You were probably not even aware of the eye movement that noted that the clef signs were in the arrangement where you as a keyboard player have usually found them (see Figure 2–4). The time signature will, if seen, also require its turn in focus. We use the expression "to take note" of something, by which we mean that we delay our reading or seeing long enough for our long-term memory, that multifaceted complex of electricity and chemistry and soul, to reinforce the schema that has been received and to make sure, by rapid repetition, that this particular configuration is not tossed out with the short-term memory bath.

If you are a more advanced musician, the propinquity of the time signature and the first three notes of the treble part will help your reading. First you will classify the information about to be received as being in a rapid 2/2; then, noting the relationship of the three notes to the barline, you will think/feel a strong beat and play/hear three notes after it, stretching evenly toward the down-beat. It would be possible that the three notes constitute a triplet, but triplets in 2/2 are so rare in your experience that you may not think of such a possibility at all, as in Figure 2–5.

Another possibility, at many stages of musical development, is that your eyes also took in the staccato markings over those first three notes the first time the saccade took them to that point. If the dots were not seen instantaneously with the notes, however, they still might have a chance to be assimilated in time to be heard in the imagination or to be played. Just as reading out loud is slower than silent reading for the vast majority of people, the reproduction of a phrase of music, either by auditory imaging or by muscular repro-duction, will take longer. If we were to play this passage at a met-ronome marking of 90 to the half note, a half measure would last for one-third of a second; the outside limit of the time it would take to read a half-measure group, however, would be one-fifth of a second, and could easily be half that required for reproduction. Thus, a vertical saccade could pick up the dots even after the notes were seen.

This leads us to two further important facts about our reading process. One is that we deal most frequently not with one but with two lines of music. Such a task will almost certainly require many such vertical leaps, as well as solid training and habituation in dealing with configurations on the page that occupy a field much broader than a single line of letters in our language (or a single column of characters in Chinese). We can in this respect seem al-most as much related to a painter looking at a bed of flowers or a human figure as we are to a person reading the morning newspaper. This is not really an accurate description, however, as we are deal-ing with a language and a grammar as well as with contours. If music were only contour, we could play any sort of ascent at the beginning of the Beethoven Rondo, anywhere on the keyboard. He has limited our choices, however, to two main configurations: G–C–D–E flat in a particular range, and the scale steps 5–1–2–3 in C minor.

The second important fact that needs to be stated at this point is that our system of musical notation is richer and more layered than our system of word notation. We have devised a way of writing down not only the relative rise and fall of pitch levels but also their relative duration in time, often accompanied on the page with instructions about their relative articulation (a form of time division) and their relative loudness. In addition, shorthand clues about the grammar of the music are embedded in clef signs, key signatures, and time signatures.[3] This is not to say that the task of reading music is so complex as to be impossible; on the contrary, the notation we have has been arrived at by historical process and offers the brain numerous advantageous shortcuts for its task of deciphering and organizing.

Simply stated, the conclusion that can be drawn from these observations about reading is this: the more you know, the more you learn. The more we can learn of the historically founded grammar of our music, the easier it is to read, just the same as it is easier for us to read *King Lear* if we have already made the acquaintance of English grammar. Beethoven's Sonata Opus 13 will be much easier for you to read if you know about chord progressions, scales, Haydn, Mozart, and other compositions by Beethoven. Here, then, is a summary of the clues we have received in starting to read this brief passage:

1. Rondo
2. Beethoven
3. *Allegro*
4. Treble and bass clefs
5. Three flats
6. 2/2
7. Eighth-note, quarter-note, and dotted quarter-note divisions in 2/2
8. C minor tonality
9. C minor scale(s)
10. Tonic and dominant harmonies in C minor
11. *piano*
12. *staccato* and *legato*

We could spend a long time discussing the various aspects of these few bars of Beethoven's music theoretically—the contrapuntal division into treble and bass lines, each with its own line or clef, the grace notes, the tonic pedal point in measure 1 as a deviation from the expected norm—but I think it would be better to take a few minutes to read another musical snippet: a phrase from the *Phantasiestücke* of Robert Schumann (Exercise 2–2).

---

[3] In this context it is easy to understand why printed music should be arranged spatially so that intervallic equivalencies are observed—a third should always occupy the same span in order to simplify the decoding process of the eyes and brain. The efforts of many twentieth-century composers to arrange groups of notes or pauses spatially is an interesting and useful way of giving the reader clues appropriate to the musical language.

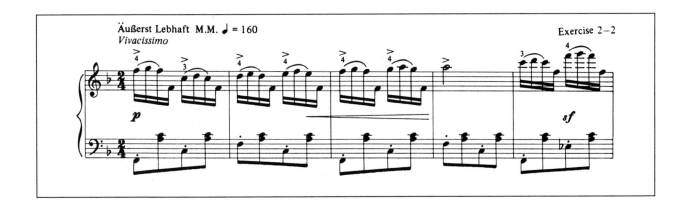

EXERCISE 2–2. ROBERT SCHUMANN,
"TRAUMES-WIRREN," OPUS 12, NO. 7.

The metronome marking is quite fast; even if we played at 150 to the quarter note rather than 160, we would finish five beats of music within two seconds, or one measure of music in four-fifths of a second. Thus the saccades, occurring five times a second, correspond to the *time* it takes to play two sixteenth notes, but, as one focus encompasses something like four or five characters/words, and short-term memory lasts only a fifth of a second, the eye is still moving about twice as fast as the fingers—which are flying!

Look at the metronome marking, the tempo indication, the clef signs, the key signature, and the time signature, set up a beat in your mind, and then quickly play the phrase on a table- or desktop. Do you observe how quickly the brain assimilates and organizes? There is no way that you could have focused on each individual note in each hand, but the brain reads according to contour, grammar, and whatever other clues it has learned to expect. There is an important lesson to be learned here: let your mind do its work.

Next, quickly go to a piano and play the message. Do not sit there and figure out the details. Do not arrange your hands. Simply, as quickly as possible, reproduce the auditory image that you have already, without thinking about it, formed of this phrase.

It is amazing how well the human brain has been arranged to do such complex tasks. If you got to the keyboard fast enough in this experiment, you probably did quite well. If, however, you had too much time to think, you may have noted the leaps in the left hand and told yourself to look out for such difficult things, thus assuring that you would miss some of them. On the other hand, if you were trying to play a bunch of notes in the F-major triad—notes that you could hear, relatively speaking—your chances were much better of being accurate. If you had time to think "I can't play this fast," your right-hand fingers may have turned to spaghetti. If, on the other hand, you were trying to reproduce a group of sounds that arranged themselves in ascending order along the F-major scale (or within the key of F major), and didn't worry about the weakness of your fingers, they probably did better than you might have given them credit for.

The point I am trying to make here is that self-confidence is not only a good psychological ploy, it is also called for and appropriate in approaching the business of reading. The brain is magnificently set up to read and to govern eye–hand coordination.

If you cannot sightread music well at your instrument, there can be many reasons. There is the possibility that you do not yet have enough musical knowledge—scales, harmonies, normal functions of harmonies, typical examples of various historical styles. If you do not have enough knowledge, then you will have less freedom. There is a strong possibility that you have a series of learned inhibitions that make you terrified of hitting wrong notes. This sort of terror might be stated baldly thus: it is better to stop and give up rather than to make an incorrect sound. I hope that you can begin to see that this is self-defeating and impractical. Another possibility is that there are some technical deficiencies that inhibit your fluency. The strongest possibility of all, however, is that you are not making use of even a small fraction of the knowledge already available to you, waiting in the form of *schemata* in the long-term memory of your brain. Your brain is ready; all you need to do is use it properly.

As we start to use the exercises and drills in the book, keep emphasizing the positive aspects of your quest. You are starting to improve your sightreading ability. The fact that you are more mature as you undertake this task is a positive one and holds out a great deal of promise and hope. Now that you have heard a large amount of music, have studied some sort of theory, and have at least the start of a musical vocabulary, you are well-prepared and ready.

One aspect of playing at the keyboard that will not be addressed frequently in this volume is hand position, or fingering. Students at a certain stage of modest advancement have to deal with the fact that, although they have learned five-finger positions on the keys, composers jump around with blatant disregard for such positions. For a few months, beginning students are apt to stop playing when the music switches hand position, look down at their hands, move to a new position, and then resume playing. When we are sightreading, however, we cannot afford to insert these pauses into the flow of the music. There are also, in commonly used musical vocabulary, groupings of notes that do not fit under a five-finger scale pattern. To take a simple example, in movements in 6/8 meter, Mozart frequently writes groups of six sixteenth notes. When we study such a passage, we must learn to accept the fact that the thumb is going to have to play somewhere in the middle of the group and that we may have to play the thumb twice in some configurations. In the exercises, games, and drills in this book we will concentrate on the notes themselves and let the fingering fend for itself. If there are fingerings printed in the music, fine; if not, we will proceed as easily as we can. We hope that our hands reach for groups of notes that are logical and comfortable, but if they do not, then we must hop or slide or do whatever is necessary to keep the music flowing.

Chapter 3

EXERCISES IN RHYTHMIC STABILITY AND HARMONIC ANALYSIS

The exercises in this chapter are designed to help you establish rhythmic and harmonic security in the music you play. First, the rhythm; the sense of pulse is the basis on which all music must rest. Music is nothing until it takes place in time. A painting remains the same at all times, static and unchanging; a novel lives outside of our time frame, waiting forever at the point where we laid it down; but music needs to be set in motion and can truly be said to exist only in a time stream. We must therefore honor the demands of the flow of time and develop a strong sense of rhythmic security.

DOWNBEAT DRILLS

The first four exercises are designed to be played as duets. The necessity of playing in an ensemble with someone has obvious benefits in underlining the importance of a steady pulse.

EXERCISE 3–1. SELECTING DOWNBEAT MATERIAL FROM A PIECE OF MUSIC

One student should be prepared to play through part of a piece that he or she knows well, while a second student sits at a second piano with the music.[1] As student A plays through the section, student B should first

---

[1] If the first pianist doesn't have the piece memorized, you will obviously need two copies.

· play only the bass note that occurs on each downbeat, striking it in unison with pianist A. It is not necessary to play the correct lengths of the notes; a short touch will do. Have a second go-around, in which pianist B should

· play only the soprano notes that fall on downbeats. A third time through, pianist B should

· play both soprano and bass downbeats.

After three times through, move on to a new page and repeat the procedure. On this page pianist B should start to play both soprano and bass downbeats immediately, if possible. The second time through pianist B can try to play the complete chord or group of notes that falls on the downbeat; the third time through, he or she should attempt to play the entire soprano and bass lines plus the chords or harmonies that fall on the downbeats.

If you, as pianist B, have trouble waiting around for the downbeats, you may need to count quietly to yourself (*one*–two–three . . .) or to conduct a beat pattern with your free hand. It is absolutely necessary to develop a sense of steadiness in your rhythm; barlines usually come along at very regular intervals, and you need to be aware of them. Try this exercise a second time, using a metronome. This may be inhibiting to pianist A, but his or her reactions are only of secondary importance; more to the point is to discover if the metronome helps or hinders pianist B.

The rest of the class can remain active by (1) conducting the beat pattern, (2) touching a surface with a finger on every downbeat, or (3) gesturing in arcs with the entire phrase or subphrase. The last exercise helps to remind everyone of the rhythmic counterpoint involved in almost all music: phrase units do not always correspond with barlines and downbeats, but can be of irregular lengths as a counterbalance to the regularity of the bars.

EXERCISE 3–2. SELECTING DOWNBEAT MATERIAL IN A NEW PIECE

Have two students sit at two pianos, each with a copy of example 1, "Melodie" by Robert Schumann. Have someone set the tempo (anyone in the room will do), and have both players start, playing only what falls on the downbeat. Keep this up for about half of the composition, counting as steadily as possible; then one person can start playing all of the right-hand part while the other plays the notes for the left hand.

As you wait through those stretches of time between downbeats, there are several features you can make yourself aware of. Some of these have to do with the actions of your eyes and hands.

How quickly do your eyes move on to the next downbeat? Do you look over immediately after striking one chord or note? Do you look over *before* you strike the chord or note, thus playing one downbeat while looking at the next?

Move on to example 4, "Stückchen." Start again with only the bass downbeat notes; try also to make your eyes leap ahead to the next downbeat as soon as possible. Halfway through the piece, add the soprano notes that come on the downbeats.

Finally, choose a third piece of music of similar difficulty and repeat the exercise.

Here is a list of points to consider; they apply to pianist B in the first exercise and to both pianists in the second one.

· Do you follow the entire musical text, or do you skip from downbeat to downbeat if that is all you are required to do at the moment?
· Does the downbeat material imply a melodic outline? A harmonic outline?
· Are there shifts of hand position that need to be addressed before you can play one of the lines fluently?
· Can you recognize shifts in hand position before they occur?
· Can you hear harmonies as the music goes by? Can you name them?
· Do you recognize harmonies as C, G^7, etc., or as tonic, dominant, etc.?
· Can you often predict what harmony will come next?
· Can you often predict what melody note or motive will come next?
· Does the metronome help or hinder?
· Does one hand need more attention than the other?

STUTTERING AND STAMMERING

One serious problem that besets pianists when we are reading is our tendency to play as if music were only a succession of notes without any rhythmic grid underlying them. If left to our own devices, we will often wait while our brain processes information and our eyes recheck details, and the result is jerky, hesitating, and incomprehensible. If we play something by fits and starts, everything we play after the first hitch in the rhythm is actually wrong. We may have played the composition correctly up to the point where we first balked, but after that it is no longer the piece that the composer wrote. Everything from that point on, whether the right pitches or not, is actually offset by some degree of time. If, on the other hand, we miss a few notes, but keep the rhythmic framework stable throughout the composition, recovering after the mistakes and putting the next notes in their correct places in the hierarchy of the form, then we are really playing the piece that the composer wrote and intended—with the exception of a few notes here and there.

Another bad habit we are likely to get into, usually out of a sincere and laudable desire to hit all the right notes, is that of stuttering or stammering. When we hit a wrong note or chord, we immediately repeat that particular beat of the music until we "get it right." This may take one repetition or a dozen, but we seem to be stuck, like a person who stammers, in our search for a particular sound, until it finally emerges from the impasse. Sometimes this habit takes the form of sitting on a comfortable chord until we have achieved a positive identification of the next one; then—and only then—do we proceed. We must always guard against falling into these habits of stammering and stuttering. We must learn to keep the beat, arranging what we can see around the rhythmic framework, and leaving out details rather than impeding the progress of the music.

EXERCISE 3–3. EXTRACTING VARIOUS ELEMENTS FROM A PIECE OF MUSIC

While student A plays a page or two from a piece that he/she knows, student B reads a copy of the music at a second piano, playing various features of the music in unison with player A. These features can be selected by the teacher and could include such facets as:

· all tonic bass notes
· all dominant bass notes
· all implied tonic chords
· all implied dominant chords
· all leading tones
· all melody lines
· all occurrences of a particular melodic contour.

Use your imagination in deciding what to outline, and include some contrapuntal (pianist B can bring out fugal entrances) and nontonal repertoire along with more traditional fare.

EXERCISE 3–4. EXTRACTING HARMONIC MATERIAL

This exercise will concentrate on the harmonies that a composer uses in a given piece. Pianist A should prepare example 7, "Marche" by Johann Sebastian Bach, and play it in class, keeping the rhythm steady. Pianist B will simultaneously play the harmonic underpinning of the music.

1. The first time through, play the roots of as many chords as possible, catching at least the bass or the root of each harmony on the downbeat.
2. Next, play the entire chord of which these notes are the roots.
3. The third time through, try to play all of the harmonies in the piece, in block form, as a background to pianist A's rendition.

Next, try this drill with a simple piece of pianist A's choice by Mozart, Haydn, or Beethoven. Are the harmonies easier or harder to decipher than those in the Bach? What are some of the differences in harmonic usage?

If you wish, try the exercise with a third piece of your choice. Do not write anything down; this will help you to recognize quickly what the composer is doing in a piece of music.

EXERCISE 3–5. PRIORITIES FOR READING

Now is the time to establish a hierarchy of steps to follow in reading a new piece of music. Turn to example 14, a folk song arranged by Bartók. Go through the following steps in sequence, patiently and thoroughly.

1.   Check the title, tempo, clef, key, and time indications.
2.   Start counting to yourself.
3.   Keeping good time, play only the bass notes on each downbeat.
4.   Go through a second time, playing everything that falls on the downbeat.
5.   Repeat this, while checking the contours between the downbeats to see if there will be any difficult shifts of hand position or stretches.
6.   Go through a fourth time, adding the melody.
7.   Go through a fifth time, adding as many bass notes as possible.
8.   On the sixth repetition, try to play all the notes.
9.   On the seventh repetition, add the articulations: phrasings, rests, cutoffs, staccati, accents, etc.
10. One last time, observe all of the dynamic and expression marks, trying for an interpretation that has expressiveness and a sense of direction.

Now sit back and grade yourself on this exercise.

- Were you able to have every note added by the time you got to step 7?
- If you messed something up, were you able to keep the beat, or did you stop?
- If you left out some facets of the music, what were they? Did you alter any of the rhythms?
- At what step did you start memorizing the music?
- What stuck in your mind first—harmonies, melodies, sequences? What remained the least accessible?
- Could you feel the relationship of quarters and halves easily?
- Was it harder or easier to read when the melody was in the left hand?
- Did chord progressions start to stick in your mind?

Take note of what seem to be your strengths and weaknesses. Are you more harmonically oriented? Is melody more important? Rhythm? What flows of its own, and what is foreign to you?

Now look at example 19, one of Mendelssohn's *Songs Without Words*. This certainly looks more complex on the page because of the continuous sixteenth notes. Go through the sequence again, and then ask yourself the questions in the preceding paragraph, plus a few more:

- Was the complex "look" of the page distracting? How? In a general uneasiness, or could you actually see too much in a single glance?
- At what point could you add the third voice?
- When could you add the ornaments? Did they disturb the rhythmic flow?
- Was the hand division in measures 29–39 confusing?
- Were the sharps and flats a help or a hindrance? Could you use them to help gain a sense of modulating? Were you able to hear and/or name triads and seventh chords when they included altered tones?
- Could you keep the relationship of larger rhythms to subdivisions clear?
- Did you use the metronome? If so, how was it helpful?

EXERCISE 3–6. PRIORITIES FOR READING, EMPHASIZING HARMONIC ANALYSIS

This time the emphasis will be more on harmonic understanding. For this purpose, turn to example 10, "Mignon" by Robert Schumann.

1. Check the tempo, clef, key, and time indications.
2. Starting counting to yourself.
3. Play the soprano and bass notes that fall on the downbeats.
4. The second time through, play the harmony that is written or implied on each downbeat, while still keeping the count steady.
5. The third time through, play these chords plus the bass line.
6. The fourth time, play the harmonic progressions of the piece; try not to omit any of the implied harmonies.
7. The fifth time, try for all the notes.
8. If you wish to go through the piece again, try to add the articulations and dynamics, and strive for a sense of direction and expression.

Next, go through this sequence with example 30, "Starlight" from Edward MacDowell's *Sea Pieces*. MacDowell's musical language is freer than Schumann's but not so much so that you will not be able to recognize triads and seventh chords. Notice also how often the music is really in two voices; the octave doubling only makes it look more complex.

If you wish, go through this drill with another composition, then ask yourself the following questions:

· What "language" did you use in thinking about the chords—G, C diminished 7th, etc.? I, iii, etc.? Tonic, dominant?
· Did you find yourself remembering some bits of information from a theory course? Take time to share them with the class.
· Was your awareness of harmonies more automatic than conscious?
· Did you allow the rhythm to suffer when you had to play harmonies that were not written out?
· Did the harmonic underpinning help move the music forward?
· How soon did you start memorizing?
· Did harmonic awareness help your memory?

EXERCISE 3–7. READING RHYTHMS ONLY

This exercise once again emphasizes the rhythmic element. Choose one of the Baroque pieces, examples 26 through 29. Set the music up on the rack and close the keyboard cover. Speak through the soprano line, not trying for intervallic accuracy but concentrating on the rhythms and using some neutral syllable such as "ta" or "la." Next, do the same for the bass. Is the rhythm that you see before you clear in your mind? Can you reproduce it orally?

Now "play" through the piece on the key cover, concentrating on rhythmic security. We often sit around "playing" on whatever surface is handy; now is your chance to do it as a class project.

Better yet, you can play this piece now without any fear of hitting wrong notes. This fear is often so all-encompassing that it blots out any sense of rhythm, line, content, or cohesion; worse, it stifles all our joy and enthusiasm, effectively substituting a negative force—fear—for the positive ones of courage and love. Sightreaders especially have to fight against the debilitating effects of this fear all the time. When fear threatens, we must find other points of focus and concentration: the flow, the architecture, and the drama of the music need our attention, not a lot of worry about a few nicks and cuts here and there. In performing this exercise, try to listen to the rhythms the composer has given—that's all you need to do.

After you have drummed through the selection a couple of times to hear and comprehend the rhythms, do not go back and try to play it with the keys uncovered; leave it only partially imagined in your mind. You can come back sometime in the future and see what the pitches sound like; for the present, however, I want to free you from fear and to instill in its place a sense of rhythmic stability.

EXAMPLE 3–8. READING HARMONIC BACKGROUND ONLY

Choose a different one from this group of Baroque examples (26–29), again setting the music up on the rack.

1. Sitting at the piano, without writing anything down, look through the composition, analyzing it harmonically. You don't need to worry about Roman numerals for the time being if that language is not natural; just say something like, "That's an F chord; then there's C major; that must be the dominant."

2. Once you have scanned the piece in this fashion, check your beginning shorthand signals (tempo, clef, key, time) and start reading. Make sure that the harmonic background remains a high priority.

3. After reading a section or a page, have everyone in the class try to sing the roots with you. If you are working alone, sing these notes yourself as you play. Can you hear the chords wanting to move forward into the next harmonies? Can you predict where the chords want to resolve?

4. A third time, try to phrase the music so that the harmonies progress into each other. Can you hear some harmonies as more tense and others as more relaxed?

Exercises 3–1 through 3–8 have concentrated on two basic skills of musicianship: rhythmic dependability and harmonic understanding. You have also worked on building up a hierarchy of values to consider when sightreading. Remember, you can jettison the ornaments or the articulations or the dynamics, but you can never abandon the rhythmic grid. You can leave out secondary voices and subdivisions of beats, but you cannot leave out the downbeats. The priorities I have listed in exercises 3–5 and 3–6 should hold true for everything you read; if need be, abandon those aspects of the music which are in sixth or seventh place, but always retain the material that is ranked first or second.

Before you leave this chapter, review the drills by working through as many of the examples from 1 through 30 as time allows. Make sure that, at some point, you read the duets by Franz Schubert (examples 24 and 25). If there is time, find more four-hand music, as the ensemble required will help keep you rhythmically aware and honest. Determine what your particular strengths and weaknesses are. You or your teacher can look for material that challenges you to improve your weak areas, be they rhythmic, harmonic, or physical. If someone in the class has more trouble with harmonic analysis than rhythm, perhaps someone else has the opposite problem, and duets and simultaneous playing of selections could be useful to both. Above all, don't go on to material that is likely to be over your head until you feel secure.

Chapter 4

TOPOGRAPHICAL EXERCISES

There are several points at which sightreading at a keyboard differs, however slightly, from sightreading on most other instruments. The shape of our instruments is peculiar, when you think about it: all our available pitches are arranged in one row, with only a slight, albeit "black and white," variance in their spacing. Compare this to the four different strings of the violin, the octave keys of woodwinds, the arcana of overtones available to brass players, and, most mysterious of all, the human throat. Each octave's worth of twelve pitches is the same size, arranged in front of us at a ninety-degree angle to our bodies. The arrangement is somewhat mechanical and quite precise.

The next few exercises focus on our physical relationship to the keyboard; they deal more with maneuverability than with music, and I think of them more as games than as drills.

EXERCISE 4–1. AVOIDING LOOKING AT THE KEYBOARD

Select a piece of medium difficulty, along the lines of examples 18–32, or something similar from the additional material. After you have checked the six initial clues—composer, title, tempo, clefs, key, and meter—stare at the first bar so intently that you can see only that section of the page; whatever you do, don't look down at your hands.[1] Without looking down, put your hands over the correct notes. Now, play them.

· Were you, in fact, correct?
· What could you feel on the keyboard that helped you to become oriented?

---

[1] If a student really can't help peeking, the teacher or another student may have to hold a screen of some sort, such as a page of music or a scarf, between the player's head and hands until he or she starts to realize some sort of control.

Without looking down, correct any mistake in the opening hand position, then play through the piece for as long as you can without looking at your hands.

· Can you keep your head level?
· Does keeping your head up tense you and inhibit you technically? If it does, tell yourself to remain calm, relax your shoulders, and breathe normally. This takes considerable control, but it is worth it. The music stand doesn't jump around; if we are trying to read what is on it, there is no reason why our head should be jerked around either.

There is also no necessity for looking down at your hands every second. This habit may be a product of that old fear of missing notes. Perhaps now is the time to break the news to you: you will miss a lot of notes in your life. You cannot escape this fact. And none but the most sadistic pseudoteacher is going to jump up and inflict bodily harm upon you. So relax!

Good sightreaders have trained themselves, either consciously or by a long period of subconscious accommodation, not to look at their hands except in the most extreme circumstances. They save themselves a good amount of time by doing so. If you remember that one-twentieth of a second is necessary for a saccade, but one-fifth of a second is needed for reading the configurations in front of the eyes, then you can see that a large percentage of time that could have been used for deciphering the notes on the page is wasted when we look away.

EXERCISE 4–2. FINDING NOTES AND CHORDS AROUND THE KEYBOARD

Center yourself well at the keyboard. Close your eyes (or, if that makes you dizzy, look up toward the ceiling), and play all the Cs on the piano. Now play all the Fs; start at the bottom and, by groping for the configuration of three black notes, work your way to the top. Now play all the A flats from top to bottom. Next, try as many E-major triads as you can find.

Next, play a pitch, for example D, in the center of the keyboard. Listen to the sound; imagine all the other Ds resounding with it. Play the middle D again, then try jumping up an octave, up two octaves, up three octaves. Does the auditory imaging help you? Try the same with your left hand jumping down.

Next, open your eyes, but keep your gaze on the music rack, so that your vision of your hands is only peripheral. Try the same drills again, playing Bs or Gs all over the keyboard, then triads in the same manner. Again, try a note or chord centered on the keyboard, listen to the sound, and try jumping up and down by octaves.

I know it may be hard for you to believe, but your brain knows where to go. The saccades of your eyes and the similar motions of your hands arrive at their goals without any muscular control and conscious dictation from you. The main goal of this particular exercise is the building or reinforcing of trust in your brain's capabilities.

EXERCISE 4–3. OCTAVE DISPLACEMENT

The person who is going to play for this game should set a simple piece, such as one of the Schumann selections (examples 1, 2, 3, 4, 9, 10, 20, or 21), on the music rack and check out the initial signs. The teacher, or a colleague from the class, should stand directly in the pianist's line of vision and hold up his or her hands vertically, palms facing each other and about six inches apart. The player will start to play. At irregular intervals the "conductor" will give signals by moving a hand to the right or the left. If the right hand (which the player sees to his or her left) moves out from the body (a motion that is then perceived as something in the field of vision moving left), the player will as quickly as possible jump the left hand down an octave and play there until that hand gives the signal to return to the middle. Similarly, a movement of the colleague's left hand to the left will cause the player's right hand to jump up an octave.

The helper can move the hands apart or together in contrary motion and can also move the hands parallel; in each case, as soon and with as little thought as possible, the pianist will respond by shifting octaves.

After playing a page or two in this fashion, try another selection in which two octaves are jumped each time a signal is given.

Here are some questions for the player:

· Can you keep your fingers supple and curved as your arm transports them around the keyboard? Try to leap like a cat, supple and graceful, and extend your "claws" only when you arrive at your destination.[2]

· Can you keep the rhythm steady?

· Do you find yourself tensing up and trying to guide your leaps?

· What is harder—parallel or contrary motion?

· Do you feel where the black-note groups are located?

---

[2] This is a parallel event to the saccade of the eye, which is followed by a moment of focusing.

· Does an octave always feel like an octave?
· Are you more comfortable in the middle of the keyboard?

LAYOUT OF THE PAGE

Not only the topography of the keyboard but also the geography of a page of music can give us trouble when we are sightreading. The next games deal with some of the troublesome topography we frequently encounter in musical notation.

Some of the examples in this book have been selected because they contain passages that ascend or descend into territory that necessitates the use of ledger lines. These areas above or below the staff can frequently give us trouble in our reading. In dealing with ledger lines you have undoubtedly already assimilated into your schemata of knowledge the A, B, and C above the treble clef and the E, D, and C below the bass, and these notes give you no more trouble than A = 440, or Middle C (which is, of course, a special ledger-line note as well). The same is probably true for the E and G above Middle C when written in the bass clef, and the A and F below it when written in treble. Further afield, however, we are likely to get lost without some well-considered and well-practiced landmarks. Learn to recognize third-line G at a glance, sitting way up there astride the fourth ledger line above the treble, and further learn to relate the high fourth-line C to it, up there a fourth higher. A fourth, your brain knows well, is always a line plus a space away, no matter where it occurs. Similarly, you can familiarize yourself with Contra F and its neighbor a fourth below, the lowest C on the keyboard. I try to rely on the Cs, Fs, and Gs among the ledger-line notes; you may discover in the course of this drill that you have acquired your own personal signposts without knowing it.

EXERCISE 4–4. LEDGER LINES

Look at example 19, from Mendelssohn's *Songs Without Words*. Starting at the beginning, read the left hand part only for four lines. Then go to the second page and read the left hand only of the last three lines.

· Did five-finger hand positions help you read the notes?
· Did the contours of the figures help you?
· Do you feel that you know F above the bass clef, for example, or A below it, automatically—that is, as well as you know the notes within the bass clef?

· Did the harmonies help you read the notes above the bass clef? Below it?
· Did the spacing of intervals, such as fifths at the beginning and octaves at the end, help your reading?

Next, look at example 32, from "Hjemve" by Edvard Grieg. Here, almost the entire right-hand part is located above the treble clef. After reading, ask yourself the same questions. Also, is there a point, such as measures 10–15, where you can no longer read quickly and need to write in the names of pitches?

Read through this selection a second time, playing the left hand as well. Does this help, or does it complicate the reading process?

Find two or three additional passages that stay below or above the staff, and read only those lines that remain there. Try to remember where the high G and the low F are. It does little good to have to count up by thirds every time the music ascends into the stratosphere.

· Do you find yourself depending on contour to help you?
· Can you play thirds and fourths with reasonable accuracy when they are written below or above the staff?
· Does it help to have a G or an F to refer to?

When most pianists get further afield than a fifth above or below a staff, they usually give up and write letter names in the music. There is nothing wrong with this; we are here to realize a composition, not to wrack our brains. There are, however, many times when dependence on contours and signposts will serve us just as well as a written "E" or "G flat." On the other hand, in the case of manuscripts where more modern composers are intent upon exploring the widest pitch ranges possible, and where, furthermore, the inexact hand of the copyist cannot guarantee that the ledger lines will be equidistant and proportional to those in a printed staff, we can feel free to write in anything we want in order to help us read the music.

The next two exercises focus attention on the shift from line to line and on the move from page to page. The backward leap from line to line can be made with great efficiency by our eyes; we must remember, however, like the television or radio announcer who must keep the flow of a sentence going, that what we are reproducing is linked in time, and the rhythmic undergirding may not falter as we move from line to line on the page.

EXERCISE 4–5. CHANGING LINES

Examples 35 and 36, the beginnings of two different movements by Johann Sebastian Bach, have been arranged so that each line contains only one measure. Get a good beat going and read down the page as steadily as possible. After you have reached the bottom of a page, stop and assess your effort. Could you really tell if your beat remained steady as you went from line to line? Check with the other members of the class to see if your impression was accurate. If your colleagues say that your beat wobbled, try the page again.

· Does it help to count aloud?
· Does it help to subdivide?
· Would a metronome help?
· Do you have to leave out notes at the end of a line in order to keep going? How many? Both hands?
· Do you land at the beginning of the new line with one hand or two?
· Can you keep your head quiet while moving from line to line?

After an assessment of any problems, proceed to another page, concentrating more intensely on the rhythmic flow and steadiness of the music.

EXERCISE 4–6. TURNING PAGES

Select a piece that you know moderately well but have not yet memorized. Play through a few pages, turning your own pages as you do so. Do you think that you kept the rhythm steady? Do your classmates agree? Try it again. Keep your breathing steady and calm, flowing with the music. How many beats before the end of the page are you ready to turn? Is your page turning ambidextrous, or do you always use one hand? Try using both in turn—whichever hand is less busy during the last measure of a page can do the job quite well.

Assess your sense of rhythmic security with the same questions you asked in Exercise 4–5. When you can achieve steadiness in the pulse while turning a page, you can be confident that you are paying good attention to the musical values of a passage rather than merely to the kinesthetic ones.

Next, have one of your colleagues turn the pages for you. Page turners can be a great help in performance, or they can be so distracting that you start concentrating on them rather than the music.

· Does the page turner wait until the last note is played before turning? This means that he or she is only listening. It would be more useful if the page turner imagined that he or she were also playing the music.

· Can the two of you find an identical pace of reading, so that both are ready to turn at the same time?

· If the page turner turns too early, can you fake the rest of the bottom measures?

· If the page turner is too late, how long does it take for you to get on track at the top of the page? Can you invent something to keep the rhythm flowing?

Most professional accompanists, if they employ page turners, will mark their music with instructions to turn early, turn late, or, at the end of a piece, DON'T TURN! Nevertheless, most of them can tell horror stories about their page turners. One of my favorite experiences along this line occurred one night in a small town in Germany when my page turner had been appointed by the mayor's office. Upon reaching the concert hall I discovered that the young man was not only no musician, he could not even read music. Luckily, the evening's fare was a song recital, so he could follow the texts, but we arranged a signal for all eventualities. I knew that the singer I was to accompany would not appreciate a lot of head bobbing on my part, so I told my turner to place his right foot next to my left, as close as was discreet, and at the next-to-last measure of every page, I gave him a quick, sharp poke on his bunions!

Once a friend of mine, while studying conducting in Vienna, applied for a job as a coach at the Staatsoper. The first selection he was given to read was the Triumphal Scene from Verdi's *Aïda*. He thought he was doing quite well, but after only two pages he was stopped and informed that he was not ready to coach. When he asked why, the forceful reply was, "Sir, you can't turn the pages in time."

EXERCISE 4–7. COVERING PART OF THE PAGE

A drill often used in experiments with sightreading involves a moving screen that blocks the player's view of part of the page. For the purposes of this exercise, turn to example 9 or 21. You might also use the C-Major Prelude from the first volume of Bach's *Well-Tempered Clavier*. Have a colleague stand to your left with a plain white piece of paper. He or she will hold the lower right corner of it in front of the music as you play, hiding the music in the following manner: as you play the first note of each measure, he or she will immediately, with a jerk, cover the entire measure with the piece of paper. Using the lower right-hand corner of the paper will enable you to see the next line of music when you come to the right of the page (as long as your collaborator doesn't get an arm in the way).

This sort of game confirms the fact that we look at what we read in groups and that the eyes leap from cluster to cluster and from clump to clump rather than proceeding one letter or one note at a time.

Next, have your partner move the paper earlier; in the case of the Bach one measure will do, but in the Schumann Etude a measure and a half can be attempted. What is your particular delay time, the gap between what you are seeing and what you can hear? Can you organize the music in groups this way?

Next, try either example 18 or 20, or a similar composition that has a large amount of motivic repetition but is slightly more complex than the first Schumann selections. Can you assimilate in groups in this music? Can you and your partner agree on what a good length of time for a group is? The partner, of course, needs to be looking at the music as if he/she were playing it; this will help coordinate the delay times.

Next, try this exercise with example 19, the *Song Without Words* by Mendelssohn. You have already heard and read this piece in class in connection with other drills; does memory and a sense of harmonic familiarity help you to flesh out what you cannot see?

There are a couple of variations on the moving-paper exercise that are curious but that I find less useful. The paper manipulator can also try to move the edge of the paper steadily across the page as you play, always remaining about a second ahead of you. I find that this version of the game usually results in heightened panic on the part of the player ("Help! The guillotine is falling!") and a complete focus on his or her part upon that shadow which is moving so inexorably and threateningly. Another possible variant is to have the paper mover stand to the right and become an uncoverer rather than a coverer. As you play the downbeat of each measure, the following measure (the one a measure in advance of the one you just started) will be revealed. My experience with this exercise makes me feel that its main result is heightened tension rather than some useful discovery. I think we need the peripheral vision of what is coming next and the sense of security afforded by being able to glance about as we are playing; there seems to be no particular reason to take it away, except as a demonstration of how we read by bunches, organizing and "schemataizing."

EXERCISE 4–8. REVIEW

For a review of how well you are doing with your reading, have two students sit at two pianos with two copies of some reasonably easy material. Anything from examples 1 through 34 will do quite well. As the piece is read, each player should, at will, (1) change octaves,

(2) leave out one hand, (3) play only the chordal background, (4) play every other beat—or any other madness he or she might decide to incorporate from the first fifteen exercises. The beat must remain steady and the flow of the music unbroken. Can you discern some particular skill that is still lagging behind the others? If so, take time to practice it on your own.

Chapter 5

COUNTERPOINT

Another way in which our reading is different from that of most other musicians is that at most times we are playing what amounts to counterpoint, kinesthetically as well as musically. Our two hands normally do not move in parallel motion; they perform two contrasting but cooperative motions. Even if the composer writes something in parallel octaves, the motion of our hands is not parallel, but opposite. Our hands are attached to our bodies symmetrically; what goes up on the right side is, strictly speaking, "paralleled" by what goes down on the left. Passages in strict contrary motion are less frequent than those in musically parallel lines (causing the fingers to work in opposite directions) or in musically independent lines (causing the hands to perform independent motions). These problems are usually first encountered by students learning their scales; solving them is the rationale for the assignment of those scales and of contrapuntal material at an early age.

Most of the time we tend to divide music into *melody* and *accompaniment*. We devote a lot of practice time to "bringing out the melody," or voicing, and we usually follow some sort of tune when we are listening. The assumption that there is one leading voice is true in most cases; it also helps define the tasks of our two hands on most occasions. We are, as I have stated before, unusually ambidextrous among musicians, and we may even feel a small twinge of envy when playing chamber music at the fact that we have so many more notes than everyone else.

If we are to become good sightreaders we must deal with reading more complex music and the broad field of vision required for seeing it. This will often involve dependence on our peripheral vision. In addition, a high degree of harmonic, or "theoretical," knowledge is required in order to synthesize two or three lines simultaneously. Truly contrapuntal music with two or more equal voices is rarely ever playable by ear; it follows, then, that such music is less easy to fake or to flesh out with our imagination. Both our brain and our eyes must be especially nimble if we are to accomplish the task of sightreading multiline compositions. It is much easier to read a chorale by Bach than one of his fugues; in the chorale we can guess the harmonic grammar. Sometime we try to read contrapuntal music slice by slice, as a succession of harmonies. We soon rebel at the illogic of such a practice, however, and fall back on two main helps: the use of our peripheral vision, and the fact that we learn various parts of a new piece at varying speeds.

The next exercises deal with, first, trying to focus on a broad band of images and, next, the problem of performing independent motions simultaneously with the hands. Then there will be a short examination of how we may combine memory with reading in contrapuntal material.

EXERCISE 5–1. PERIPHERAL VISION AND PRIOR KNOWLEDGE

Take a piece of paper and a pen or pencil and write a paragraph. It can be a description, a letter to a friend—anything. After you have written four or five lines, freeze, stopping the point of the pen or pencil on the paper. Look fixedly at the word you have just written. Then, *without looking up*, observe the shapes of the words two lines above that word.

· Can you recognize these words?
· Do the dimly seen shapes recall what you have written? If not, leap upward and back as rapidly as possible, gazing for the length of one saccade on one particular shape from that higher line. Continue the exercise, making sure that you don't peek, stopping occasionally to test the strength of your peripheral vision.
· Which is more important in recognizing those words above, peripheral vision or memory?
· Do these two attributes help one another?

EXERCISE 5–2. TWO-VOICE COUNTERPOINT

Even in the simplest music the secondary voice may be more melodic than we might give it credit for. Read examples 4, 20, and 30 again, observing how your focus on the right-hand melody is continually distracted by the contours of the left-hand part. Notice, as well, how the melody is indeed the part that gets the most attention.

What we call peripheral vision is as much subject to the commands of the brain as is the intent stare that focuses on a single object. In both cases we are searching for clues and configurations that will connect with our previous experience, and in both cases we will try to accomplish this connection as rapidly as possible. We cannot command our eyes to focus on two things at once; we always deal with a foreground and a background. As you look at a page you are also aware of the color of your clothes, the shapes of furniture around you, and other such configurations out of your range of focus. If an altogether new object were to enter your periphery, you would register two things: first, its sudden appearance and, second, the fact that it was not a part of your cumulative learned experience or, in other words, your memory.

EXERCISE 5–3. PARALLEL VOICES

There are also many passages, of course, where the two hands double each other. In example 85, passages from the Trio by Bohuslav Martinů, there is a great deal of parallel writing. In example 88c, a passage from the Quintet by Verne Reynolds, the hands start out in octaves and then proceed to parallel motion at other intervals. Read these two sections.

· Can you keep looking at one hand and have the other follow along subconsciously?
· Do you focus on the right-hand material? Does this mean that your left hand is used to following more automatically and unconsciously?
· Do you stare at the lower, or left-hand, part? Is this because you have an easier time with the right-handed line?
· Does your brain accept the information that a long line in octaves does indeed remain equidistant?
· Does the distance between the lines on the two staves help this concept?
· Do the contours help keep the octaves equidistant? Do the accidentals?

EXERCISE 5–4. LEADING WITH THE LEFT HAND

Find a piece of music, such as example 14, 15, 18, or 22, in which the left-hand part is quite interesting. As you read it, try to command your attention to the lower line to the exclusion of the upper.

· Can you see the right-hand staff peripherally?
· Do you find it necessary to leap vertically with your eyes?
· Is it easier or harder for you to read music in which the left hand has the leading voice?

- Do you think this results from years of accommodation on the part of the brain to expecting the melody to appear above the accompaniment?
- Is it because you have not practiced enough to gain technical fluency with your left hand?
- Is it because of some innate attributes of the two hands?

EXERCISE 5–5. FOCUSING ON ONE VOICE AT A TIME

Find a two-voice composition that is definitely contrapuntal in nature, such as the easier pieces of J. S. Bach; examples 5–8 will do fine, or you can find others. The first time you read through it, focus on the upper voice as much as possible. The second time, switch your attention to the lower one. Can you start to recognize features in the upper line peripherally, or do you have to bounce your eyes up and down?

Select another such two-voice composition, and read only the top line through, twice. Then add the lower voice. Does this process make it easier to see the upper part peripherally? This method attempts to place one voice further along in the process of learning than the other, so that your attention could be directed more toward new material, leaving the more familiar parts to be jogged out of your memory. At what point in the process of repetition does one figure or phrase start to be memorized? Thereafter, can you recognize this with minimum effort so that you can concentrate on the more elusive features of the music?

EXERCISE 5–6. THREE-VOICE COUNTERPOINT

Find something written in three voices, such as found in the pieces by Johann Kirnberger, examples 27a, b, or d. The first time you read the piece, try to make the top voice as complete and accurate as possible, while faking the lower voices. Repeat this until the top voice is secure, then read the selection with your focus on the bottom voice. Repeat this until both top and bottom are well learned. Now try this with one of Bach's Three-Part Inventions.

- Do you find that the middle voice came along without being invited? Is the music complex enough that you need equal time for the middle voice as well?

· In the simple Kirnberger pieces, is it easier to think of the middle voice as belonging to either soprano or bass, rather than as an independent entity?

· Do you reduce the three voices to two entities, one for the right hand and one for the left?

· Can you observe what it is that your eyes select as foreground and background as they read the page?

· Can you observe your brain operating on several levels, combining elements that are memorized with those which are newer and less familiar?

In conclusion: there are two practices that are of great help in reading the dreaded monster, counterpoint. One is to operate as if you are looking at foreground and background. Focus on one line and leave the other to peripheral vision. (This does not mean that you will always look at the right hand or the treble clef, however; you may find that your primary focus will switch back and forth several times during the course of a single passage.) The second method is quite similar, with the foreground and background occurring in time rather than space. It is of great help to many people to read one hand or one line in advance of reading the entire texture of the composition, thus making that part of the music more familiar and more readily assigned to peripheral vision.

Contrapuntal music is never easy to read *prima vista*. Remember, however, that almost all the music that we keyboardists read and play is contrapuntal to some extent. It is therefore necessary for us to work at it, organizing passages into hierarchies of melody and accompaniment, foreground and background, focus and periphery.

Chapter 6

IMPROVISATION

In this chapter we will explore further that aspect of playing music (and sightreading) that is often referred to as "faking." You may be aware that jazz musicians call the collection of harmonic and melodic sketches out of which they learn and play their repertoire a fake book. These musicians are not seeking a sloppy approximation; their fake book enables them to analyze and synthesize the tunes they play with maximum accuracy. Being purveyors of the art of jazz, moreover, they have maximum freedom to improvise and are engaged in creating music rather than playing a series of notes.

It may be more appealing to call the skill that we practice in these exercises improvisation rather than faking. When it comes right down to it, however, and we are sightreading in a pressure situation, a certain ability to fake the details is a useful commodity. You may, upon reflection, have noticed how often you have engaged in this fine art of approximation when you have been sightreading, filling out inner voices by some sort of harmonic guesswork, completing scale passages without looking at every note, or playing by ear rather than checking every detail on the page.

This series of exercises, similar to those in chapter 4, can be thought of as games rather than drills. When we are improvising, there is a wide margin for correctness, instead of the wide margin for error we are used to contending with. There are many possibilities latent in every musical situation, and the judgment of what sounds better in a situation can be based on appropriateness of style and grammar rather than faithful reproduction of what is on the page. Take time to listen supportively to each other's improvisations, voicing opinions on what sounds most pleasing, or most inventive, or most like the music of some particular composer. As you make these judgments, take time also to examine the basis on which you make them. Is it personal taste? Familiarity with a certain composer's style? Theoretical knowledge?

EXERCISE 6–1. IMPROVISING MOZART

You will need some cooperation in preparing the music for this exercise. Each student will be working with a melody line by Wolfgang Amadeus Mozart; he/she should be able to see the melody line only, without the accompaniment. It should also be a work with which the student is not familiar. As each student will need only the melody line, another student or teacher might use the violin or voice part that has no piano accompaniment written with it or an appropriate selection with the left hand (or accompanying instrumental part) covered with a piece of paper. The end result should be a melody from Mozart with no accompaniment, and each student's piece should be prepared for reading by someone else.

1. Read through this melodic line once, listening attentively and analyzing it as well as you can.

   · What sort of harmonies are outlined?
   · What harmonies seem to be implied?
   · What sort of cadences?
   · How often do the harmonies seem to change?
   · What spirit or mood does the music seem to represent? Is it driving, languorous, capricious?

2. Next, play the passage again, and without thinking too much about it beforehand, play something with your left hand to go along with Mozart's melody. Only when you have finished should you stop to consider what you have done.

   · What did you play—chords, arpeggios, single notes, Alberti bass figures?
   · Could you keep the left hand going all the time?
   · Did you choose appropriate harmonies?

   If you made a mess at times, you should be very happy, because you had actually dared to do something original rather than hanging back and mistrusting yourself.

3. Next, take time to think about and discuss what sort of figures Mozart uses for his accompaniments. Play some repeated eighth-note figures, some simple outlines in octaves such as 1–3–5–8 in quarter notes, some simple arpeggios in various arrangements, some Alberti bass figures, some tremolos.

4. Now, and only now, take away the paper, look at the passage the way Mozart wrote it, and see what he uses in this instance.

   · Are his choices predictable or surprising?
   · What energy level does his choice of accompaniment bring to the music that it did not possess as a naked melody?
   · What sort of accompaniment figures might supply more drive? More smoothness? More solidity?

Now that you have thought more deeply about these issues, have another Mozart passage chosen for you. Again hiding the accompaniment, play through the melody while analyzing the harmonies and gestures of the music. Make some educated choices about appropriate accompaniment figures, the speed of the harmonic changes, and the level of complexity of the music. Then play your version of Mozart's tune, combining his right hand with your underpinning. How did you do this second time? I'm not expecting you to be another Mozart—that's impossible for anyone—but his style is as familiar on the one hand as it is inimitable on the other, so you can easily judge how well your improvisation succeeded in its goal to "sound like Mozart."

If you wish to have another Mozart game, try improvising your own imitation Mozart melody. Have an accompaniment passage chosen for you, analyze the harmonies, and try to make up a melody to go with it.

If this is fun, try making up the start of a Mozartean sonata-allegro movement. Without writing anything down, invent a first theme, play a few phrases in that spirit (perhaps employing some scheme that has question-and-answer phrases), and then modulate to the dominant key.

This sort of improvisation in a particular style may seem to you to have very little to do with sightreading. It is, however, closely related in two important ways. First, very few of us can see all the notes of every composition the first time around; and so, if we are not to break down rhythmically, we have to fill in the blanks out of our own memory-inspired inventiveness. Second, the human brain reads by scanning for clues that fit into schemata that, in turn, fit in its vocabulary. The more we know what to expect in Mozart, the better we can read a new piece by him. I used to amaze people when I was in college by sightreading a new sonata by Hindemith with relative ease. This was, however, after I had already worked on two of his viola sonatas, a violin sonata, a horn sonata, and other pieces, so that the style was becoming a part of my experience. Of course, it will almost always be easier for a musician to read Schubert than Schoenberg: "common practice" chord progressions are part of our education, while atonality, by definition, seeks to break apart the rules of grammar we have spent years learning.

EXERCISE 6–2. IMPROVISING BAROQUE MUSIC

Select a movement from a suite by Johann Sebastian Bach or Georg Friedrich Handel, or, if you have not yet read it, one of the less familiar Baroque selections from examples 26–29. Be sure to choose material that is new to you. It will help if the movement is a dance of some sort, with a recognizable rhythm. Read through the movement as well as you can, observing how the composer has put his music together.

· What sort of cadences are used, and how frequently?
· How often do the harmonies change?
· How many voices are there?
· Does the number of voices change? When?
· What motivic figures are used, and how frequently?

After you have played through the piece, go back and check those features I have mentioned again, assuring yourself that you understand the construction of the music, the texture, and the sort of figures that the composer has chosen. Then, on the second run-through, read what is written only as far as the first cadence; after that, improvise the next section, trying to match and balance what Bach, Handel, or one of their contemporaries has done in the first section. If this goes well, keep on going, shaping your improvisation to have the same number of phrases or sections as the original and to have the same sort of modulations with a similar frequency of harmonic changes.

· Could you find the correct notes with your left hand for the harmonies you heard?
· Could you hear the harmonies you wanted or only name them?
· What sort of figures did you actually use?
· Could you keep both hands moving all of the time?

Now try it again. Don't be discouraged if you play a lot of dissonances; it is much worse if you stop and start on every beat. Keep going, no matter what it may sound like.

What do you find difficult about this late Baroque style? The frequency of the harmonic motion? The intricacy of the rhythm? The counterpoint? Can you juggle more than one line at a time?

EXERCISE 6–3. IMPROVISING BRAHMS

Find a selection by Johannes Brahms that you don't know. Choose something chordal from the songs or the shorter piano works. (Remember, a chordal passage needn't look like block chords on the page; Brahms uses a lot of arpeggiated figures in his piano writing, and such a passage will do very well for this exercise.) Play through the piece as well as you can, getting used to the feel of the texture and the density of the harmonies.[1] After one reading for familiarization with the topography, read it through again right away, looking more carefully at the compositional choices.

· How frequently do the harmonies change?
· How many seventh chords are there? What kinds?
· What sort of melodic motives are used?
· How constant are the rhythmic devices?

Next, it is your turn to compose. Invent a harmonic progression of three or four chords that sounds Brahmsian. Fool around until you get something that appeals to you. Then place a melodic figure over it. You may not like the first thing that comes, so adjust it until you have a phrase that you can use as a starting point. Then proceed to develop your idea, spinning things out and altering them in what seems to you to be a Brahmsian style. Try to use the structure employed in your model. If Brahms answers four-bar phrases with four-bar phrases, try to do that. If he elides or extends his phrases, try to do the same. If Brahms keeps a steady flow of eighth notes, try to do likewise.

· Could you think up consequent phrases that answered what you had just played?
· Could you find sequential melodic contours?
· Could your hands find the chord members needed to provide the accompaniment figures?

A list of features that might be considered in determining what makes a composer's style personal and unique would include the following:

MELODY AND GESTURE

    length of phrase
    length of line
    contour (reversing or one-directional)
    derivative or imitative devices
    ornaments
    embellishing notes on or off important beats

HARMONY

    typical progressions
    frequency and type of seventh chords

[1] If the thought of sightreading a piece by Brahms dismays you, look for one of the simpler songs, such as *Wiegenlied* or *Sapphische Ode.*

chromaticism
normal versus unusual functions
quartal harmonies
polytonality

RHYTHM

repeated motives
complex juxtapositions
polyrhythms
stretches of the same note value
arrangement of phrases and periods

TEXTURE

chordal
homophonic
arpeggios
counterpoint
accompaniment patterns

EXERCISE 6–4. FURTHER IMPROVISATIONS

I hope you are getting interested in "fooling around" at the keyboard. Improvising is, as you can see, a useful tool in gaining mobility and ease with the music you are called upon to read. I also hope you can see that it can be a lot of fun. Here are some suggestions for further improvisations. Choose one or two of them, find a model to listen to, and then try your hand at it. In each case, consult the list above and take time to determine exactly what it is that makes the music of the composer sound authentic, whether it is harmonic usage, texture, rhythmic flow, or some other feature.

1. A description of a landscape: Debussy
2. A nocturne: Chopin
3. A chorus: Handel
4. A theme with variations: Beethoven
5. A ballet movement: Stravinsky
6. A dramatic encounter: Wagner
7. A strophic song: Schubert
8. A water piece: Liszt

9. A water piece: Ravel
10. A romantic ballad: Gershwin
11. A folk song: Copland
12. An allegro: Hindemith
13. A romantic interlude: Tchaikovsky
14. A humorous song: Poulenc
15. A sarcastic dance: Shostakovitch
16. An operatic aria: Verdi
17. A description of birds: Messiaen
18. A description of motion: Glass

Any exercises of this sort can help you in a number of ways. Working on them will sharpen your skills at analysis; it will free you up at the keyboard; it will make it easier to fill in secondary parts when reading; and it will help you gravitate more naturally to correct and appropriate harmonies and figures when reading. Above all, you will start to discover secrets of style that will enable you to play authoritatively and convincingly.

Chapter 7

TRANSPOSING

Now we are going to discuss and practice a skill that intimidates—even terrorizes—many musicians. This skill is *transposing*, or the act of playing something in one key when it has been written on the page in another.

There are many good reasons why keyboard players need to practice transposing and add this skill to their other abilities. For example, singers often need to take a song up or down a key in order to make it fit comfortably within the compass of their voice, and they are within their rights to expect that we oblige them. This is just as true for mature stars as it is for grade-school choruses. You may have observed that many songs are published in high, medium, and low keys to facilitate finding a comfortable key for most singers, but there are lots of times when the range of a particular song will not agree with the range of a particular voice. In the case of most opera arias, almost all oratorio selections, and some sections of certain song cycles, it is traditional to keep the selection in the key in which the composer wrote it. In most cases, however, there really is not particular ground for staying in the written key. Indeed, most audiences would certainly prefer to hear a comfortable singer singing well, hitting notes with ease and pronouncing the text with clarity, rather than be forced to sit through a rendition full of squalling or growling that is undertaken for the sake of "textual faithfulness."

Another practical application of transposing is that it stretches and expands your ability to analyze and think while the music is in progress. If you employ methods of transposing that emphasize analysis and listening, it will certainly end up helping your sight-reading.

Most professional accompanists will be able to tell you stories about times when they have had to transpose in public. Several major vocal artists (not just in the distant past, either) have been in the habit of asking their pianists to take everything on the program down a tone if "the voice" is feeling tired. There is a story, perhaps apocryphal, that Chaliapin, after the first selection in a recital, would give a discreet signal to his accompanist if he wanted lower keys for the rest of the evening. After the first few concerts of a tour where the signal was invariably given, the pianist had a brainstorm. He played the first song of the concert *up* a key. As he expected, Chaliapin felt "uncomfortable," gave the signal, and the pianist read the remainder of the concert in the printed keys, saving himself a great deal of extra work. What's more, the basso never noticed the difference!

There are several techniques that can be employed when transposing, and I would like you to try all of them in order to find what works best for you. You will probably find that you will end up with a mixture of various techniques, which will be far from being a disadvantage. If you think how complex the act of playing music at a keyboard is, an act that you perform constantly, then it is only logical that you are capable of learning a complex schema for the act of transposition as well.

EXERCISE 7–1. TRANSPOSING BY EAR

The first of these various skills to try is the simplest in concept and may very well prove to be the most useful of all: playing something in a new key by ear. Take one of the examples 1–21 that you have heard frequently in class. Play the first note anywhere on the keyboard but where it is written, decide what key you have placed yourself in, and see if you can remember what comes next. Of course, you will probably find that it is easier to maneuver in C major or G major than in F sharp minor. Don't feel guilty about that; if you need to figure out a comfortable key to transpose into, do so—it will certainly help your analytical skills. If you have some luck with your first endeavor, try the selection in a third key, and then another. Do you notice yourself starting to memorize the piece, albeit in a slightly skewed fashion?

Next, try the same thing with some simple piece you know by memory. Start it by ear in some other key, and see how far you can go. After the first breakdown, try to start up again and keep on going. You will most certainly notice the conflict between tactile signals (I am supposed to put my first finger on F sharp!) and auditory ones (the contour of the melody goes up *this* far now), and you will also start to notice the importance of the chord progressions more with each repetition. There may be a point at which you start trusting the way music sounds rather than how it feels,[1] and you will start relying on logic rather than chance. If so, you will have made an important transition from being primarily a "groper" on the keyboard to being a true listener to the music you play.

---

[1] Music will, of course, always have a strong tactile hold on the performer—just think of how most singers approach music—but a life spent concentrating on mechanical reproduction of a series of actions rather than listening to what is to be created in sound seems a pretty poor trade-off.

EXERCISE 7–2. TRANSPOSING FAMILIAR
MELODIES BY EAR

For this drill, look at example 44, a familiar old folk song of Great Britain and America called "The Nightingale." First, read the song in the printed key of C major. Next, play a second verse in D-flat major, then a third verse in D major. After you have completed three verses, the class should see if a volunteer can sit down and play the song in a key other than the printed one, transposing *prima vista*.

· Can you, the first pianist, remember the tune well enough after one read-through?
· Were you accurate on the larger intervals such as the sixths?
· Which intervals were the easiest to remember?
· Could you relate the two tonic notes (an octave apart) to each other and stay within the tonality?
· Does the switch from white to black notes confuse you?
· Are the contours of D-flat major less familiar than those of C major?
· How far could the second pianist remember the tune?
· Were there intervals that remained incomprehensible to him/ her?

If "The Nightingale" or "Barb'ry Allan" are completely unfamiliar to you, perhaps you can find other examples of folk songs or folklike melodies to test your ability to remember and transpose melodic lines.

Next, look at one of the two Stephen Foster songs (examples 42 and 43). Play through the song you have chosen once, familiarizing yourself with the melodic contours and the harmonic structure. Then play the song three times, rising a half step with each verse. Thus, "Beautiful Dreamer" will be in E flat, E, and F, while "Old Folks at Home" will be in D, E flat, and E.

This sort of skill depends to some degree on what sort of theory training you have had; it is often easier to play a chord progression if you can think about it before you play it. This is not always true, however, and in the interior battle between the brain's desire to recognize and identify everything around it and the personality's nervousness about trusting itself to do the right thing, a continual conscious effort to name a series of harmonies is often exhausting. The ability to play by ear develops along with the knowledge, to be sure, of how music is put together; this knowledge, however, is not simply restricted to what we learn in a theory class. I am quite sure that research would show that those children who have had training in theory and analysis are likely to be superior sightreaders.

Research also shows, however, that children learn a lot about music by listening to good performances of good music. After a teacher has pointed out the importance of an authentic cadence, the transition at the beginning of the fourth movement of Beethoven's Symphony No. 5 becomes even more overwhelming and satisfying; after the shift of mode from major to minor is grasped, Schubert can break your heart.

The ability to play by ear owes a great deal to a sense of appropriateness that helps you judge and select harmonies at a level close to the threshold of conscious thought. Most jazz musicians and church organists have learned their theory lessons very well and have also practiced and repeated these lessons so much that dexterity and fluidity seem more a function of reflex than of will, even if they have never had a formal theory lesson in their lives; their schoolroom has been the music that they have listened to attentively and sensitively. This continual listening process is a good practice for all of us to cultivate and will be helpful in many different situations. I don't recommend that you try to go into a trance and wait for a chord to strike you; a little trust in what you have heard and learned, however, would prove to be very useful. If we are capable of listening to music, both before and after we play it, we will have help when our memory falters or when there are too many notes on the page for us to grasp.

The second student in exercise 7–1, for example, did not get a chance to read the song in the proper key. Is there a way to go directly from your auditory imagery to the touch of the fingers on the keys? This sounds like a subject diametrically opposed to sight-reading, doesn't it? I am convinced, however, that people who play well by ear can learn to sightread well and that there should be no artificial boundaries set up in how people respond to and re-create music.

READING THE C CLEF

We keyboard players have gotten used to reading in two different clefs, the treble and the bass. If, however, you look through the thousands of orchestral scores that you can find in a library or music store, or borrow a trombonist's or violist's music, you will see that many musicians seem to be at home with the C clef. Examples 55–68 have lines in various clefs, and you can find plenty of C-clef reading there (as well as in the other scores and parts mentioned on pages 79–87). Three particular C clefs are encountered frequently. The tenor clef is used by cellists, bassoonists, and trombonists, as well as by tenors reading Baroque music, and the clef sign brackets middle C by framing the second line from the top. The alto clef, with the middle C sign bracketing the middle line of the staff, is used most frequently by viola players. The soprano clef, where middle C is on the bottom line, is most frequently encountered in soprano parts in Baroque music.

EXERCISE 7–3. TRANSPOSING USING C CLEFS

Look at the parts in example 56, the Chorale "Nun danket Alle Gott" by Johann Sebastian Bach, to see how we can familiarize ourselves with lines written in C clef. First, try to compare the look of these lines with the look of the treble and bass clefs you know so well. The alto clef, for example, has a C one interval lower than the C you find in the treble clef (space down to line), and one interval higher than the C you find in the bass clef (space up to line).

1. Read the alto line as if you were reading treble clef, but playing up a step; you have to remember, however, to play the line in a lower octave. (Although it is what you are actually doing, saying that you are transposing down a seventh sounds too complicated!)
2. Similarly, pretend to be reading bass clef, but pull everything down a step—in a higher octave.
3. Next, read the tenor line, which starts on A, as if you were reading treble clef, but pull each note down a step.
4. Finally, read the soprano line, which starts on E, as if it were written on treble clef; you will have to pull each note down a third.

    ·   What happens between B and C, between E and F?
    ·   Can you keep a tonal sense as you transpose the melody this way?
    ·   Can you envision the use of these pseudoclefs being a tool that, if practiced, could help you master C clefs?

5. Paint yourself an imaginary red line along the line that is designated middle C. Read the alto part, using this as a continual point of reference: "Now I am a third above middle C, now I am a fourth below it," etc.[2]
6. Read the tenor line (or the tenor line of another chorale, if you have this one memorized) while keeping the second line from the top fixed in your consciousness as middle C.

---

[2] In the alto clef the notes that fall in the spaces beyond the first ledger lines both above and below are also Cs and can also be used as constant points of reference. Just as our double staff of treble and bass is symmetrical in regard to the Cs on a grand scale, the alto clef is symmetrical on a smaller scale.

· Can you keep the pitches straight using this method, or is it too cerebral for you?

· Do you find yourself forgetting which clef you are reading?

· Does this "fixed *do*" system hold out promise of being a viable method for you to use in conquering C clefs?

7. Finally, try a third method. Figure out what note one of the C-clef melodies starts on, check what key you are in, and read through the part horizontally. If the line goes up by steps, do the same from wherever you are located; if the line descends a fourth, perform the same size jump. This is a technique frequently employed by singers, dealing as they do with a single line and an instrument without keys or frets; they find such intervallic reading especially useful when there is no strong tonal center.

· Is this a comfortable method for you?

· Do your ears tell you if you get off and land on the wrong scale-step?

· Can you keep a tonal sense while juggling the intervals?

If you are a member of a class, take some time for a discussion after everyone has tried all three methods of dealing with the C clefs. Is there one of these three, substitution of clef signs, a fixed *do* reference, or intervallic line-following, that makes the most sense? Is the class vote split or unanimous? Is there one method for you personally, no matter what the vote may have been, that seems the most promising? Did you, even in the few minutes devoted to the exercise, see that you might be able to combine elements of all three methods, sometimes following the contour of the line, sometimes noticing where C is, and sometimes transposing?

After some time for thought and discussion, go back and select some more lines to read, checking your own thought processes as you do so. As with all the exercises, spend enough time on this project to learn something. Don't just play with a subject long enough to convince yourself that you are ignorant; stick with it until the light begins to dawn! It is hard to set time limits on a subject as varied as musical performance, and sightreading is no exception. If the class is ready to move on and and you are not, then you should add clef reading to the list of things that you must practice frequently.

You may wish to talk to bassoonists or trombonists and find out how they deal with the C clefs in their music and how they shift back and forth. You, however, will not use the C clef as frequently as they will and thus will not have the kinesthetic drill in its practice that they have. We should not, however, excuse ourselves from learning how to read C clefs at all. We could get through a quintet rehearsal without knowing exactly what the violist and cellist are playing, just as we could accompany Russian songs without being able to read the Cyrillic alphabet; it is not a very safe feeling, however, and smacks of ignorance and sloth. A good conductor must read all clefs, and a good chamber music player need do no less. You will find that most of the best musicians in the business, the ones with stability and self-confidence and informed viewpoints, regard clef reading as a tool of self-evident importance, whose mastery, once practiced, is a trifle in the overwhelming stream of musical knowledge.

EXERCISE 7–4. TRANSPOSING BY INTERVAL

This exercise explores another method of transposition, one that does not go by any neat title. It is sometimes referred to as transposition by interval; I frequently refer to it as *nudging*, because you take what you see and nudge it up or down by a certain interval. Take one of the simpler examples such as 1–32 and, without playing it as written, play it up a major second. Every note, every chord, and every figure that you see must be nudged up a step. Be careful to keep within a key; accidentals will be a problem, so you will have to think more sharply when they appear.

This exercise should feel dangerous, as if you are living on the cutting edge. Using this method of transposition rather than playing by ear is almost like simultaneous translation; it is as if a diplomatic translator had to speak one word at a time. Even now, however, you will start to notice that your brain's habit of forming schemata will start to operate, and you will be nudging groups of notes rather than individual ones.

Next, try transposing another simple selection down a whole step. Is there any difference in your ability to move up or down?

Next, try some section of music up and down a major third. After you have attempted this, introduce a method that hearkens back to exercise 7–3: see if you can, by an act of imagination, displace the lines and spaces you see, moving them down in your mind so that E becomes C, G becomes E, and so forth. Imagine that there is one less line at the top of the staff and one more at the bottom. Now try to read the passage a third higher than the composer wrote. Does this creation of a pseudoclef help? Which helps you more, pure transposition by nudging or the image of a pseudoclef?

EXERCISE 7–5. TRANSPOSING BY CHANGING KEY SIGNATURE

Find some examples that are written in the key of C, such as 1, 2, and 4. Select one and play it in the key of C sharp. All you have to do in this case to transpose is simply change the key signature in your mind (not neglecting B sharp and E sharp). Accidentals are relatively easy to think about: a sharp becomes a double sharp, a natural becomes a sharp, and a flat becomes a natural—everything moves up one degree. Next find a simple piece in D, such as example 7, and play it in D flat. Here your thought process is redirected downward: sharps become naturals, naturals become flats, and flats become double flats. You won't find many F naturals or C naturals in the key of D, but they will become Es and Bs.

See if you can find more pieces of music that you can transpose by changing the key signature—E to E flat, A to A flat, and so on. Then tackle a piece in E, nudging it up to F. Here the accidentals may drive you crazy. When moving between B and C or between F and E it is usually a lot simpler to play by ear than to try to figure out a system that sorts out the many enharmonic spellings that are involved.

EXERCISE 7–6. TRANSPOSING BY VARIOUS METHODS

Select another music example and try out all four methods of transposition discussed.

1. Start by playing the first note of the melody up a fourth and follow the contour of the line horizontally for a few measures.
2. Then try to nudge everything up a fourth as it comes.
3. Then read the next few measures as if C were on the second line from the bottom in the upper system, and the Cs in the lower system were on the bottom line and the top space.
4. After this, go back to the beginning and try faking your way through what you have read so far, playing by ear in the key that is a fourth higher than the printed one.

    ·   What specific situations can you discern in which one or the other method will prove the most useful?
    ·   Are you starting to have a personal favorite?
    ·   Does music that consists mainly of melody and accompaniment lend itself to the use of one method?
    ·   Does chordal music? Contrapuntal music?

Many pianists who play in public find that they must occasionally use yet another method, that of memorization. They will memorize every detail of a piece in one key and then play it in another, taking enough practice time to assure themselves that they have all the details memorized in the new key.[3] Most pianists who have to transpose material, as you might suppose, will practice until the piece is well on the way to memorization; few performers want to fly blindly through a performance, although accompanists must be prepared for everything. And the way to be prepared for everything? Practice, of course.

EXERCISE 7–7. READING AND TRANSPOSING TONE-ROWS

Examples 37–41 are tone-rows from various compositions. These make good exercises for sightreading because of their unusual combinations of intervals. They are also fine exercises for transposition. Try the examples in every possible transposition, especially larger intervals such as fourths and fifths. After you choose one of the rows, do not play it as printed but start it, say, a tritone higher. Then complete the line on that level.

· What method of transposition are you using?
· Are you nudging?
· Are you following the contours?
· After you have played a row through a few times, do you arrive at a point where you can recognize the intervals before they appear?
· Are you, in fact, hearing the intervals before you play them?
· Are you forming arbitrary groupings of three or four notes ("This is almost like a major seventh chord" or "These four notes are similar to those four notes")?
· Do you notice how often these composers have actually formed their twelve-tone rows in groups of four notes, or tetrachords?
· Is there a point of which you start playing by ear? By memory?

Let me caution you not to leave the subject of transposing until you feel you are making headway. If you feel that you are not ready to move on, add a few minutes of transposition to your weekly routine. Don't leave an exercise until you understand what it can mean to you. If twice through will suffice, fine; if you need four, or six, or twenty repetitions, fine. One of the joys of all music study is its personal and individual nature. We are all proud of what comes out of our personalities; we can be just as jealous of what goes into the process of forming our minds.

---

[3] There are stories of those legendary pianists who could play all forty-eight Bach Preludes and Fugues in all keys; this feat would be the culmination of both transposing and playing by ear!

Chapter 8

SCORE READING

There are good texts and fine methods that are devised to help conductors learn how to read and deal with their scores, and I am not trying to present this subject as it relates to keyboard skills in anywhere nearly as exhaustive a manner. There are many benefits to be gained by learning to read a score easily and to play from one at the keyboard. Reading from score combines the skills of transposing, clef reading, analysis, dividing music into foreground and background, and improvisation. If you can learn to cope with orchestral and chamber music scores without flinching, you hold the key to opening the door to wonderful worlds of music, more varied and colorful than anything available to a single traditional keyboard instrument.[1]

Look at example 46, a vocal quartet by Stephen Foster. The parts for soprano, alto, tenor, and bass are written on different lines. This arrangement is used in most choral scores, whether a capella as this one is or with accompaniment.

In modern vocal scores the tenor part is written in treble clef, an octave higher than the actual pitches that the tenors sing. This transposition of an octave is the only strangeness involved in reading such a score; it is simply up to the player to remember which line is the tenor part. For example, if you look at the Monteverdi madrigals (examples 47 and 48), you will see that there are two tenor parts, while in the Verdi selection (example 49) there are groups of soloists stacked on top of two choruses, giving us parts for (reading from the top) a soprano, a mezzo, a tenor, a baritone, two basses, a mixed chorus, a male chorus, and another mixed chorus.

Transposition is not the main problem in reading scores of this sort; much more distracting is the fact that the lines are spread out over such a large distance vertically, requiring leaps of the eyes up and down as well as left to right. This makes the activity involved in reading more contrapuntal in nature than reading the "normal" two-staved piano part. There is also a sort of visual static contributed by the text or texts written in between the staffs.

---

[1] The electronic future, of course, holds promise of all sorts of new horizons in music; this will not necessarily eradicate the love of, or the need for, the traditions of "acoustic" music we have grown up with.

EXERCISE 8–1. READING AN
OPEN VOCAL SCORE

First, read several measures of the soprano, alto, and bass parts only (together) of the Foster quartet (example 46), bouncing your gaze back and forth as smoothly as possible across the expanse of vocal lines.

Next, read only the soprano, tenor, and bass parts.

Next, read only the soprano and bass lines. Your eyes will not be able to focus on both lines at once, so you will have to use foreground and background techniques. Try to read groups of soprano notes, then groups of bass notes, organizing and assimilating as you move steadily forward.

Finally, read the outer voices again, but add whatever you can fake or catch a glimpse of in the inner voices as well.

· Did the beat remain steady?

· If not, was a wide interval in the left hand to blame (tenor parts are often placed far away from bass parts, as you see seven measures from the end)?

· Was the wide spacing on the page to blame for rhythmic hesitation? Did you need extra time for your eyes to jump up and down?

· Is it harder on your eyes scanning such a tall score than one with only two lines?

· Do you have trouble with the octave displacement of the tenor voice?

· Does it confuse you when the tenor and alto parts cross? The last time around, were you able to redistribute the parts between the hands to alleviate this confusion?

Now try the same exercise on other examples of choral music. Read at least one of the Monteverdi examples (47 and 48). Then read one of the sections, vertically speaking, in the Triumphal Scene from Verdi's *Aïda* (example 49). Select either the solo group or one of the three choruses. You might want to look in scores of operas by Mozart, Rossini, and Verdi for more examples of vocal ensembles that are unpredictable in the number of sopranos or tenors or basses involved. This is usually more challenging and more fun to read than simpler choruses that are arranged SATB.

When you read a few examples of choral writing, you can always check yourself with the piano reduction written below. In a rehearsal situation, the rehearsal pianist can always play this part—until the conductor asks her or him to play only the tenor and alto parts, or to leave out the bass line, or some other rehearsal device. Then, of course, he/she will have to be able to read vocal scores in much the manner we have been drilling here.

EXERCISE 8–2. ALL-WOMEN'S AND ALL-MEN'S VOCAL SCORES

Examples 50–53 are choral selections for female or male voices only. The former are simple enough to read, as everything is in treble clef. The latter are even simpler; all you need to do is move your right hand down an octave from where it would normally read the upper (tenor) parts and play the music in close harmony. The hands keep pretty much to themselves; even if the thumbs cross, the right hand ignores the baritone line, and the left hand doesn't bother with the second tenor, and everything goes quite smoothly. Example 52 has a solo line in addition to the four-part male chorus; leave this part out at first, and then see if you can cover a significant amount of the choral parts with your left hand while reading the solo line with your right.

EXERCISE 8–3. READING MUSIC WITH OBBLIGATO INSTRUMENTS

Examples 54 and 55 are Baroque works that are written for voice, an obbligato instrument, and keyboard. You will probably be able to find many more such arrangements in the library or in the possession of a friend who is a singer. If you can get a singer to volunteer to help with this drill, it might enhance the experience; if no singer is able or willing to sing the vocal line, perhaps a classmate can play it on a second piano.

The Handel aria (example 54) has been arranged for keyboard, instrument and voice; example 55, the Bach aria, however, is reproduced here more or less as Bach wrote it, with a basso continuo line. With someone else taking responsibility for the vocal part, play through the Handel selection, reading not only the keyboard part but also the line for the obbligato instrument. When reading the Bach aria, play only the single bass line, as written.

· Can you get your eyes to jump back and forth across the intervening vocal staff?
· Can you keep the rhythmic flow?
· Can you give the singer all of the clues he or she needs in order to sing? In the Handel aria, what do you need to leave out and to include in order to arrive at a satisfactory version for keyboard alone?

Try the selection through again, making musical sense out of it, even if it is at the expense of completeness. After reading the outer voices of the Bach aria a few times, you might wish to try your hand at filling in the implied harmonies while still covering the soprano and bass lines. At first, however, concentrate on reading what is written. If you can find similar Baroque arias with instrumental obbligato, repeat the exercise with them. If there is no written harmonization of the continuo part, add some of the chordal harmonies as you read.

EXERCISE 8–4. OPEN SCORES
BY J. S. BACH

Examples 55–59 are pages from scores by Johann Sebastian Bach. If you look through them you will discover that he wrote in a variety of clefs and that he was probably as much at home in the various C clefs as we are with our treble and bass ones. To what purposes does he employ the C clef in these pages? Can you find examples of the C-clef usage that you were introduced to in the preceding chapter?

First, choose one particular line that is written in C clef, and read it through. Which method of reading are you employing—nudging, contour following, playing by ear?

Next, go back and play this line with your right hand while reading the lowest voice (whatever constitutes the bass line) with your left hand. This line may be in a gamba part, or a continuo line, or could be the lowest of the vocal parts.

· Can you keep the two staves separate in your head?
· Does the C clef tend to interfere with the bass line and pull it awry?
· Which hand is more competent?
· Can you hear the implied harmonies as you are reading?

You may feel that this drill is pushing you to go too fast, but you have been reading music at the keyboard written in two different clefs for years; why not try mixing the C clef in with that practice?

Next, go back and try to combine your original line with another voice that is also written in C clef. If the selection you have been working on has only one instrument in C clef, check out the vocal parts of the chorales; there is ample opportunity to read in soprano, alto, and tenor clef there.

Start by reading the newer C-clef line through first; then combine the two voices.

· Are you allowing your harmonic antennae to pick up clues as to what note is coming next?
· Can you improvise notes that are appropriate when you cannot transpose fast enough?

· Do you find that you can devote most of your looking to the newer voice, trusting your memory and your peripheral vision to cover the material learned first?

· Are you ready to attempt three separate lines at once? You will probably find that you need not pay much attention to the bass line by now, so that might be a good choice to include. You will also naturally feel more comfortable with three lines which are adjacent, even if they are written in three different clefs.

· After this time through the selection, have you reached a point where the piece is memorized? If not, try to add some other voice, so that you are reading bass, a familiar C-clef line, and a brand-new line, either treble or C-clef.

By now, the music you have chosen should sound quite familiar; before you leave it, therefore, try to play as good a version of the entire composition as you can. Check all of the preliminary signs once more, to give your brain all of the schemata it needs; remind yourself of what the music has sounded like in its partial form; give yourself a slow but steady beat, and play through, catching as many details and configurations as possible, while supplying the missing links from what seems appropriate at the moment.

If this is too much for you to bear, back up a few steps and try a different approach. Start with the bass and soprano on the downbeats, just as in chapter 3, and add other elements one at a time: the downbeat harmonies, those harmonies plus the bass line, the soprano line, the inner voices, and finally all of the notes on the page. If you can convince yourself to decide upon and to follow these priorities in your reading, it should always help you understand the music more quickly and reproduce it more effectively.

If you turn to examples 60–65, you will find that they are pages from various orchestral scores. The first three are from a special genre, divertimenti written by Mozart for a predominance of wind instruments, while Mendelssohn's *Ein Sommernachtstraum* employs chorus and soloists as well as orchestra. Before trying to sight-read any of the parts, take time to examine the layout of the page and some of the details. If the entire column of instruments does not fill a page, some editors will insert double slash marks on the sides separating the collective lines. In the examples included here, no such marks are included, so you might find it helpful to mark them in. For example, such marks are useful in example 60 halfway down the page in the right margin between the bass line and the oboe line.

You can see how the page is arranged by instrumental choirs, with the woodwinds on top, followed by the brasses and the violins, with the vocal parts and the remaining strings occupying the bottom of the page or line. There are few places where you may be able to find C clefs; the violas will be written in alto clef, and the trombones, bassoons, and cellos might be in tenor clef. In the centuries since Bach's time, composers have used the C clef less and less, but in scores of works by Beethoven, Berlioz, or Schumann and their contemporaries you will be able to find all sorts of clef usage that I will not have time to go into here. Scores that are reprinted facsimilies of older editions are more likely to use "old" clefs than modern ones, which may have reduced the number of transpositions from what it was in the original.

You may also notice that the various instruments seem to be in different keys. A piece might be written in F major, except that some instruments seem to be playing in D, or in B-flat, or in C. This multiplicity of key signatures results from a long process of historical development through which some instruments that are in use today have been designated "transposing" instruments; that is, the players read one pitch but play another. If you are not familiar with this phenomenon, you might profit from a conversation with a horn player, clarinetist, or oboist.

For your own purposes of sightreading, however, you only need to know what specific transpositions you will be facing. Flutes are written at what is known as "concert pitch"; that is, you read the parts right where they are written. The piccolo is written an octave lower than it sounds, and the alto flute is written a perfect fifth higher. A note written on the second space of the treble clef (A = 440) sounds right there on the flute but comes out of the piccolo an octave higher (A = 880) and out of an alto flute sounding D above middle C. Oboes do not transpose, but the English horn sounds a fifth lower than it is written.

The clarinets—ah, the clarinets!—are written either in B flat (a step higher than sounding) or in A (a minor third higher). If there is no indication in a score of which is intended, clarinets in B flat or A, you can look at the key signature. If the oboe and flute are in D, a signature of E (four sharps) on the clarinet line indicates that B-flat clarinets are in order, while a signature of F (one flat) calls for A clarinets. Then there are E-flat clarinets, written a minor third *below* the sounding pitch, and bass clarinets, which are usually written a major ninth above where they sound—and there are various other clarinets and saxophones that can be found mostly in band scores.

After the clarinet family, bassoons are a relief; they are "in C" (they sound as written), but—you can't have everything easy!—they frequently go into tenor clef. Trombone parts are just like bassoon parts, and trumpets can be either in C or in B flat (do you remember what that means?). Due to a history in which horn players changed tubing on the instrument for each key in the composition, horn parts can be written in all sorts of keys and traditionally have a no-sharp, no-flat key signature, so that they look like they are written in C major all the time. In more recent scores you will usually find the horn parts in F, that is, written a fifth higher than they sound, like the English horn and alto flute. Sometimes the key signature is without accidentals (as if it were C major), and sometimes it is that of a key a fifth higher than sounding. Notice how, in the Beethoven selection, the various instrumental choirs are connected by double lines. In the much more complex Wagner score, the horns are bracketed. In almost all scores, the first and second violin parts will be written on separate staves but will be bracketed.

EXERCISE 8–5. FULL ORCHESTRAL SCORES

Choose a page or two of one of these orchestral scores, and study it at the keyboard in the following manner.

The layout of the page:

1. Name each instrument, from top to bottom. How many of each wind instrument are there?
2. Look at the second system. If the selection you are studying is one of the Mozart divertimenti or the Beethoven symphony, this system will be on the same page with the first. Scanning from top to bottom, review the order of the instruments again. Example 63 renames the instruments in front of each system, but most scores do not, so conductors have to write notes to remind themselves which line belongs to a particular instrument after the first page.
3. Find all the transposing parts. Name each transposition—for example. "The basses play an octave lower than written"—and then play the first note of each transposing part on the keyboard.

The arrangement of the musical elements:

1. What key is your selection in?
2. What is the meter?
3. What is a reasonable tempo?
4. Scan through several measures, then play whatever you think is the main melody.

- Does it stay in the same instrument for a page or more?
- Did you have to change clefs or transpositions between phrases?
- Which is harder for you, transposing something in treble or bass clef, or reading something at pitch in C clef?

5. Find the bass line and read it. Does this stay in the same instrument? Is there a change of transposition involved?
6. Play the melody and the bass together.

If you are starting to suspect that I am leading you through the list of priorities that I established in chapter 3, you are correct. These priorities give you a framework that will help you learn the music at every step of the way. You can proceed along these lines, adding the harmonies that come on the downbeats and filling in the inner voices. You will not have reproduced every note or every detail on the page; there are simply too many notes, in most cases, to read with exactness. You will find that either your peripheral vision, or your harmonic sense, or both, will be there to help you with the details; indeed, your feel for harmonic grammar will be directing your peripheral vision as to what to look for.

EXERCISE 8–6. ORCHESTRA SCORE-READING, EMPHASIZING THE TRANSPOSITIONS

Choose a different orchestral score for this exercise. If you have been working on one of the Mozart pieces, move to one of the "taller" scores, and vice versa. Or you might find it interesting to use the full score of one of your favorite orchestral works, one that is not included in this book.

1. Name all the instruments from top to bottom, not forgetting to notice how many of each there are.
2. Find all the transposing instruments.
3. Are there parts in F—horns, English horn, etc.? If so, read them first.
4. Are there parts in B flat? If so, read them for several measures.
5. Are there clarinet parts in other transpositions? If so, read them through.
6. Which C clefs are used? If there is a viola part, read it.
7. If another instrument is written in C clef, read its line. Now that you have looked at all the hard parts, go back to step four in the preceding exercise and get acquainted with the piece of music as a whole.

EXERCISE 8–7. FULL SCORES AS DUETS

For this drill, two players should sit together at one piano with an orchestral score. Make sure you agree on key and tempo, then start reading, with the person on the right picking out the melody wherever it occurs on the page and the person on the left finding the bass and playing it. Deciding where melody and bass lines occur shouldn't take more than a second or two, once you familiarize yourself with the layout of the page. Composers are likely to use cellos, basses, or bassoons for the bass line, but the melody can fall to all sorts of instruments. The contours, however, will probably be obvious enough for you to make a good judgment of what is melodic and what is not.

After you have made an effective duet out of these two strains of music, branch out and fill in more details. If two scores are available, it is convenient to move to two pianos for this stage of the exercise. If not, the person to the right may have to play a few things up an octave. Each of the partners should choose one section of the orchestra and be responsible for those lines. One pianist could try all of the string parts, while the other manages the horns; or one could play flutes and oboes while the other handles viola and cello parts. Trade parts and sections enough so that you develop confidence in what the harmonies and the details of the music are. Then, after discussion, divide the material in some logical way between you, and try for a cohesive paraphrase of the music.

I would wager that until recently you never thought that you would be able to progress to the point where you were actually reading an orchestral score at the keyboard. And yet conductors and many other musicians use this skill all the time. When I was a student, Dr. Howard Hanson, who conducted over one hundred new scores every year, would sometimes call me into his office to help him read a new composition. I would frequently have a piano reduction, but he would sit at a second piano and play just as fast as I would—and usually a good deal more accurately—while reading out of the full orchestral score.

One of the reasons you can start to aspire to such acts of reading is simply the fact that you already know a lot of music and a lot *about* music. The mind is ready to recognize familiar signs and to make new and interesting formations out of the building blocks it has used before. All you need is a push toward exercising your mind in new skills. One of the pushes most of us respond to quickly is economic; if we know that a particular ability is necessary—or at least very useful—in making a career, we will go to great trouble to acquire it. Another great motivator is curiosity; we have all had experiences, to take an example from the world of music, when we hear a piece by some composer who is new to us, fall in love with it, and cannot wait to find as many other pieces by the composer as we can lay our hands on.

EXERCISE 8–8. READING STRING QUARTETS AND QUINTETS

By now you should be ready to do some reading in the string quartet literature. You might be puzzled that I proceed from tall orchestral scores to the intimacy of a quartet. My logic is as follows. When we read a full orchestral score, we are almost always cheating—we have to approximate, leave out parts, reduce the range, for example. This is not necessary when reading a string quartet; here we can, with a little practice, play almost everything that is written, exactly and with no compromises. The order of exercises is devised at this point to move from the approximate to the exact, not from the little to the huge.

There are many good editions you can use; the Dover reproductions are large enough to fit on a piano music rack and are large enough to be read. The Eulenburg and Kalmus pocket scores are useful for taking to concerts (with a flashlight) but usually cause us to squint if we try to play from them at the keyboard.

1. Choose either one of examples 66–68 or another quartet or quintet movement, and read it first as a duet for two pianists at two keyboards. The first time through, Pianist A will play the first violin and cello parts, while Pianist B plays second violin and viola.

2. The second time, Pianist A should play both violin parts, while Pianist B covers the two lower voices.

3. Decide which division of parts is the most comfortable, and then repeat the section until what you are playing is polished and musical.

4. Next, take turns playing the entire selection as a solo. When playing by yourself, you may again have to omit some of the details at first. You may discover, for example, that you focus most of your attention on the viola part and play the bass more or less by ear.

    ·   Which voice is most likely to get left out?
    ·   Which voice is most likely to be read incorrectly?
    ·   Are you using your harmonic sense to invent the unseen details?
    ·   Are you reading horizontally, following the contours rather than the individual pitches?
    ·   Is one of the lines always in focus, or does your point of focus move around?

Take time to discuss and to think over the various methods you have found effective in dealing with reading from a score. Decide if there is one aspect, such as harmonic imagination, that you have not utilized well enough. It could be that this particular approach is not necessary to your progress, of course; but if you suspect that it could be helpful, then you can return to some of the exercises that emphasize that aspect and drill them more carefully.

Look at the vocal parts in the Bach chorales (examples 56–59). If you can find an edition, such as the one by Riemenschneider, that has all the chorales in original clefs, this will do nicely for numerous hours of score-reading practice. These chorales present quite a different sort of quartet: here, instead of one C clef, we have three.

Start to play one of these sections also as a piano duet. If you are sitting together at one piano, the person to the left should take care of the tenor and bass parts; even so, your fingers will still get tangled up on occasion. If you can read from two scores at two pianos, you can then trade off parts so that one person can read alto and tenor, for example, while the other plays the outer voices.

Once the music starts sounding familiar and is half-memorized, each pianist can try to play all four voices alone. You will find that you need every weapon in your arsenal: harmonic know-how, horizontal-contour reading, transposition by interval, and a sense of humor that will let you keep going when all seems to be falling apart around you.

As a curiosity, you might try reading a chorale one note at a time, building up each chord from the bottom. Your process would be as follows: look, play bass, hold it; look, play tenor, hold it too; look, play alto, hold it too; look, play soprano, release; look, play bass, hold it; and so on. After a short time at this process, you will be able to see that it might be useful for checking your clef-reading skills, but it certainly will not help your musicianship in any real way or your sightreading ability in particular. You have actually graduated from such a stage and are capable of much more mature processes.

This chapter on score reading has dealt with skills and with repertoire that you might never have included in your concept of what is meant by the term "pianist." One of the most attractive aspects of the field of music, however, is its vastness, and it is always thrilling and stimulating to discover a new area and to start to explore it. Before you go very far in the field, score reading will also become practical and useful, whether you are accompanying a chorus, playing a quintet with four wind players, working on a vocal selection by Bach or Handel, or learning to conduct a great symphony.

Chapter 9

ADVANCED RHYTHMIC AND NOTATIONAL PROBLEMS

Rhythmic stability is the basis for sightreading well; if we imagine the various elements of skill that we are actively employing when we sightread to be arranged in a pyramid, the bottom layer is rhythm, supporting layers of analysis, knowledge of style, dexterity, and self-confidence. All of these skills will in turn support your attempts at fluency and accuracy.

Composers, however, do not always play fair with rhythms; throughout the history of music they have been as interested in developing new rhythmic variations and possibilities as they have found new harmonic and melodic ones. You have probably already confronted two against three in Chopin and groups of sevens and elevens in Beethoven. The music we read is full of complex subdivisions, surprising syncopations, and ingenious mixes of rhythmic elements. We must deal with all of this bounty when we read.

EXERCISE 9–1. MIXED SUBDIVISIONS

Examples 69–72, 80 and 87b feature various subdivisions of the beat. Before you tackle one or more of them at the keyboard, take time to speak through a drill, as follows. Tap a steady beat, which is represented by the vertical lines to the left in Figure 9–1, and speak a series of subdivisions within that beat, represented by the words to the right of the lines. Each line in the figure should take exactly the same amount of time.

· Are you able to make your various subdivisions equal within the beat?

· Which subdivision is the most problematic for you?

· Which pair of subdivisions?

Try mixing up the various subdivisions, leaping from two to seven, or trying five three times in a row. Remember that subdivisions are

68

Figure 9–1

69
*Advanced Rhythmic and
Notational Problems*

| one

| one-two

| one-two-three

| one-two-three-four

| one-two-three-four-five

| one-two-three-four-five-six

| one-two-three-four-five-six-seven

| one-two-three-four-five-six

| one-two-three-four five

| one-two-three-four

| one-two-three

| one-two

| one

just what the term sounds like; they are small units which fit together into larger ones, the larger ones being of constant size. Steady pulses with varying subdivisions are like city blocks of equal size, some of which contain two houses, others five, and still others only one.

EXERCISE 9–2. MORE MIXED RHYTHMS

Read through several of the musical examples listed above, and try to find some of the other musical references listed in the back of the book. Be sure to include example 72, the selection from Gluck's *Orfeo ed Euridice*, written around 1760 and still complex enough to stump all but the most practiced sightreaders.

1. Find the measures that have mixed subdivisions of the beat, and speak the rhythms aloud. There are various syllables for rhythmic reading in use; employ whatever works for you.
2. Play the complex sections on the key cover or a tabletop.
3. Establish a tempo that will work for you.
4. Read the complicated measures by themselves or in pairs.
5. Start at the beginning of the musical example, and incorporate the problematic measures into the piece.

EXERCISE 9–3. MIXED METER

Examples 73–76, and 79, as well as many works cited in the list of music for further study, contain examples of mixed meter. Sometimes a composer will ask for a simple alternation of two different measure lengths; more often the changes from one meter to another will be irregular. In example 79, the passage from the Sonata for Viola and Piano, Hindemith indicates at the beginning that the measures will either be two quarters or three quarters in length, but his pattern of switching from one to the other is irregular. At first it looks as though he has written a pattern of 2/4, 2/4, 2/4, 3/4, 3/4, but this sequence happens only twice. In such pieces as the song by Mahler (example 73), the shifts of meter between 3/4 and 4/4 help the lyrical flow of the music, especially the fluid vocal line. Example 74 from Holst's *Sāvitri* alternates 3/4 and 4/4 to produce a continuous 7/4; the composer also warns you when the sequence 3/4–4/4 is going to reverse and become 4/4–3/4

1. Speak the following rhythm patterns aloud, with each word taking one beat of a steady pulse.

   1. |one|two|three|one|two|three|four|one|two|three|one|two|three|four|one
   2. one|two|one|two|three|one|two|one|two|three|one.

   Composers will sometimes alternate the denominators of the time signatures, mixing 4/4 with 3/8 or even with 3/16, for example. The works of Orff and Stravinsky have many famous examples of this sort of technique. It is just as easy to keep the beat steady here as in the works where the quarter note represents a constant beat throughout measures of equal length; all you have to do is count the subdivisions during those measures which have the larger beats.

2. Speak the following rhythms in a similar manner, one beat per word.

   1. |one|and|two|and|three|and|four|and|one|two|one|and|two|and|three|and|four|and|one
   2. |one|two|three|one|and|two|and|one|two|three

   One measure's subdivisions become the next measure's principal beats, and vice versa.

3. Now look at example 76, the opening of Maurice Ravel's opera *L'Enfant et les Sortilèges*. Notice how Ravel's measures keep changing in a seemingly random pattern. Set a good *quarter-note* beat, and read the beginning.

4. Now look at Example 75, the second player's part to a section of *Ma Mère l'Oye*, to see how Ravel sets up definite expectations that the measures will keep getting longer within a pattern.

5. Look at example 77, Capriccio for Oboe and Piano by Jacques Murgier. Are the five eighth notes per measure arranged as three beats followed by two or as two plus three? Check your key and clef signs, decide on a comfortable tempo, and read this selection.

If this rhythm is difficult for you, count it aloud, practice it on the key cover, and then try it again.

EXERCISE 9–4. MUSIC WITHOUT BARLINES

I have included a few examples, such as the pieces by Roy Harris and Erik Satie (examples 81–84), and cited many others in the back of the book where either the barlines seem to be placed at random or there are no barlines at all. Here, of course, it does no good at all to insist on keeping barlines equidistant and steady; our thinking must be binary and sequential. It is as if we are counting "one-one-one-one-one" or "one-and-one-and-one-and" throughout the piece.

Select two of these passages to read, playing everything as a succession of equal eighth notes or quarter beats.

The Satie is relatively repetitious; you can quickly start to pick up the repetitive patterns and will be able to form schemata that are, for all intents, measures. Many passages from Benjamin Britten and Charles Ives, to cite two composers who use irregular barlines frequently, are much more complex, harmonically as well as rhythmically. Don't worry about your wrong notes for the moment; just concentrate on the steadiness of the rhythm.

Conductors, who make a living by beating out the rhythm for other musicians among other things, will take such scores as these and mark them by dividing these supermeasures into more easily digested chunks. A section between two barlines in which Britten has placed thirteen quarter notes, for example, may break down into groupings of 4 + 3 + 2 + 4. It is also a long way from the steady repetitions in Satie to Ives's "Concord" Sonata, where the accented beats are continually rearranged, or "The Cage," a song by Ives, where you can start out counting steadily in quarter notes, only to find the beat displaced by an eighth or a sixteenth.

EXERCISE 9–5. SPATIAL NOTATION

You will find that many recent composers have arranged the notes spatially on the page, as in examples 92–98. Here is a logical extension of the cadenzas that you may have already seen in Beethoven, Chopin, Liszt, or Schumann (see example 90), except that here the relation between eighths and sixteenths is more tenuous. There are frequently no stems or crossbars on the notes that could be of some use in a traditional sense. You must simply play the notes in succession in a rhythmic relationship to each other that corresponds as closely as you can devise to their proximity to each other on the page. In example 92, *Klavierstück IX*, Stockhausen writes a group of notes under one crossbar because that group is to be played as fast as possible; there are groups of varying lengths, but each is to be played with great rapidity. In the David Bedford piece (example 93), these groups of notes are further collected and arranged by the inclusion of dotted lines to direct your eyes. In Examples 93–96 dots and bars designate sounds that are to be short or to be held for a designated (or hinted at) duration.

Some composers will delineate a time frame, such as five seconds, and require the performer to fit the notes within that framework in a manner corresponding to the spatial relationships on the page; *Piano Piece 1* of David Bedford (not reprinted here) is an example of this technique.

Select one of the examples or some similar material written in a spatial format, and sightread it.

· What came easiest the first time through—pitches, rhythms, or contours?
· Which did you pick up the second time through?
· How long does it take you before the notes start being reasonably accurate?

The performer is given a certain amount of freedom and responsibility in this style; the responsibilities, however, greatly outweigh the freedoms, and detailed study reveals very careful and thorough instructions from the composer. It is hardly necessary for me to point out that (1) the fact that it is contemporary music doesn't give us the right to play anything that comes into our heads, and (2) the proper performance of such music, as for that of Beethoven or Debussy, goes far beyond the province of sightreading.

It is fun, on the other hand, to see how well you do at reading such difficult music. I have included several miscellaneous rhythmic puzzles, such as example 78, which looks easier than it is, especially if you are playing it with an oboe. You might accumulate a little list of your favorite brainteasers and, with increased familiarity, become more proficient in styles that are located far afield from Mozart or Bach. Some chord progressions will always seem new until they are memorized; but the rhythms, with practice, have a chance of becoming familiar. If you keep an eye out for rhythmic conundrums, practice them away from the keyboard by speaking or tapping them, and build up your flexibility, then it will be a delight to come across some new twist such as the last movement of Virgil Thomson's Cello Concerto, or the rhythmic modulations in the works of Elliott Carter, or the mixed-rhythm ostinati in many works by Paul Hindemith and Paul Creston. You will have come a long way from the simple downbeat drills in Exercises 3–1 through 3–8; you will not get there, however, except by the straight and narrow path through such drills. If you develop habits of steadiness and solidity in your rhythms, there are no limits to what you can do.

There are times when a composer or a copyist will give us information on the page that is misleading. Music in manuscript is likely to offend in various ways: ledger lines are not measured consistently, so that what looks like a high E in one measure is the same distance from the staff as a high G in the next; the beats that subdivide a measure are written in varying widths; notes and accidentals are placed so that they could be interpreted as belonging to either the line or the space.

Printed music can also deceive us. Clefs can change without our noticing it; slurs can be ambiguous; enharmonic spellings can trick us into moving when we should hold our ground; intervals can be something other than what they seem (E flat to C sharp, for example, looks like a third and must be consciously and laboriously relabeled to conform to its sound of a major second). Further, the composer's ideas of voice leading can cause him or her to arrange the notes on the page in ways that must be rearranged to fit the two hands. Some composers with less regard for the historical development of tonalities will spell chords in ways that may seem convenient for the alignment on the page but that cause us grief when taken in context.

EXERCISE 9–6. DECEPTIVE CONFIGURATIONS

Examples 87–98 contain many such deceptions. Work through some of them at the keyboard, marking with a pencil the specific reading problems and trying to decide if there might be a way to write them that would help your reading.

· If the ledger lines are badly aligned, draw horizontal connecting lines, or label notes with their letter names.
· If beats are unclear, draw vertical lines to help the eye.
· Label chords with their numerals or symbols.
· If the hand division is awkward, draw curves that will enclose the proper groups of notes.
· Respell notes enharmonically that are confusing.
· Label confusing intervals—most people mark a minor second with a < sign, a major second with a [, and use the labels m3, M3, P4, T, P5, m6, M6, m7, M7, and 8 to name the other intervals.

EXERCISE 9–7. DEFINING THE UNREADABLE

There will always be, for us normal mortals among musicians, some music that we will have to call unreadable. This may be due to the fault of the composer, who has asked for a complexity that borders on the physically impossible; or it may be due to a lack in our musical education. When reading such music, wherever the blame may lie, we will always feel that our process of analysis is always slower than our vision. In some music we will always feel that we are playing something that we really do not know. When working on some music, such as the Chopin "Winter Wind" Etude, the Rachmaninoff Etude in E-flat Minor, or the Debussy Etude *"pour les accords,"* to name three examples, we may have to memorize the music before we can read it, thus effectively bypassing the sight-reading process except at an extremely slow rate of speed.

Music examples 87–98 contain extreme examples of musical writing. You can find many other such pieces, either in my list of references or on your own. Select one of them and make a study of the typographical, rhythmic, harmonic, and stylistic problems that you find. Then make a presentation to the other members of the class, explaining why a particular piece is, in your opinion, actually unreadable. You might then disprove your own thesis, at least to some small degree, by playing a few moments or effects out of your chosen selection.

CONCLUSION

We must finally return to our initial question: is it possible to learn to sightread? Is it possible to read one line and leave another to peripheral vision? Is it possible to learn to play without looking at our hands? Is it possible to learn to leave out some notes while concentrating on other, more important features of the music? Is it possible to recognize the harmonies that make up a piece by looking at the page? Is it possible to learn to keep a steady pulse, no matter what our eyes and hands may have to do? As a lawyer might object, I am obviously leading my witness—and I hope that the answers are in the affirmative.

One of the basic assumptions of social psychology is that the human animal is singularly devoid of what is called instinctual behavior. Somehow, in the development of our amazing powers of deduction and communication, we have lost our reliance on those reflexive actions which we call instincts. We rely instead upon learned skills, and our brain is magnificently equipped to aid in this process. There is therefore, within what we call the normal biological range of human equipment, no such thing as a "natural reader." There are only people who know things—some more than others. Due to various causes, some people are less inhibited and more courageous than others; others are near- or farsighted; others have double-jointed fingers, or short, stubby ones; others have excellent work habits. We could make a very long list of qualities and attributes that could be considered relevant to the skills involved in sightreading; no two students would have the same profile.

The basic question must again be rephrased: can sightreading be *taught*? To back up another step, can playing the piano be taught? Here, despite the fact that thousands of people make a living teaching the piano, the answer must be: up to a certain point. Teachers can tell people about good posture and proper mechanics, can describe theoretical issues, can describe styles, can exhort and inspire and inflame, can criticize and demonstrate until blue in the face; all their effort, however, is useless, unless it is put to use by the student. You are the one who trains the muscles and disciplines the thoughts.

You must recognize the abilities that are latent in the brain; you must trust the accumulation of knowledge that you have acquired; and you must be willing to practice your skills. Sightreading is a skill, not a genetic gift; and if you do not sharpen and use it, it gets rusty very quickly. A few minutes a day will produce noticeable improvement in your abilities—this is the truth of the maxim that one learns to sightread by doing it. A few hours a week spent learning music, new or otherwise, while thinking about style, controlling your rhythm, listening to your sound and your technique, and observing the features and configurations of the music, will produce advances that you will not be able to ignore. A few hours a week in an ensemble situation, whether accompanying or in a group, and with the same care and attention, will make your skills and self-confidence evident to everyone. Given a certain level of technological proficiency, sensitivity, and dedication, these skills could develop into professional caliber.

Less than one percent of the musicians in the western world cannot read. I would venture to say that less than five percent of the working musicians in the western world cannot sightread. It is simply a necessary skill for all sorts of musicians; it helps trim hours off the learning process, and it is an important qualification for auditions and job interviews.

Further, sightreading is fun; it helps us learn music firsthand rather than having it spoon-fed to us. You all know the almost unbearable pangs of joy and wonder that you experience when listening to a great piece of music for the first time; this exhilaration is doubly present for the person who can sightread. To the thrill of discovery and the ravishment of the new and delightful are added the satisfaction and pleasure felt only by those who are actually playing. There is nothing wrong with watching a documentary about wildlife on television, but it is something quite different to explore an underwater reef or an alpine meadow firsthand. Similarly, there is nothing wrong with listening to recordings; this, however, is also passive compared to reading and playing music yourself. This is not only active but also exciting and stimulating to the mind, ear, and body; we are on the cutting edge in experiencing the art that claims our enthusiasm and our love.

If, as has been stated, our remembered experience is the most important single factor in our reading ability, then there will be some musicians who will be able to read music more quickly than others, simply because they have heard more music than others. I have found, in my own experience, that compositions that confounded me the first time I studied them became much more accessible the second time around. Thus, the first time I performed Schoenberg's *Pierrot Lunaire* I felt that I knew what was coming next only a frighteningly small percentage of the time. A year later I discovered that, even the first day I started to practice the music, many pages seemed like old friends.

We could, therefore, continue our exploration of music, seeking ever more difficult rhythms and ever more abstruse styles. I would love to compile a second anthology that you could follow into greater complexities and into greater triumphs of sightreading. I think that the principles that I have put forth thus far would remain valid, no matter how far into the music of the present or the future we might venture. It is time, therefore, for me to withdraw and leave the field to music itself, with its almost infinite capabilities and configurations, for your exploration and your delight.

Suggested Music for Further Study

Anything from the world of music could be employed as material for sightreading. Here are a few suggestions to help the student and teacher in searching for additional material.

COLLECTIONS OF RELATIVELY SIMPLE MATERIAL:

Beside collections of miscellany for beginners or modestly advanced students, there are also:

Bach, Johann Sebastian	Little Preludes and Fugues	Henle, 1959
Bach, Johann Sebastian	Notebook of Anna Magdalena	Henle, 1953

(These are good critical editions; there are many other editions in print.)

Adler, Samuel	*Gradus*	
Bartók, Béla	Mikrokosmos	Boosey & Hawkes
Bartók, Béla	Piano Music; for Children	Dover, 1981
Kabalevsky, Dmitri	24 Pieces for Children	G. Schirmer
Niles, John Jacob	Song Book for Piano	G. Schirmer
Schumann, Robert	Album for the Young	Various editions
Türk, Daniel Gottlob	49 Pieces for Beginners	Kalmus, 1950

MORE ADVANCED COLLECTIONS AND SPECIAL PIECES:

Berio, Luciano	Wasserklavier	Universal, 1971
Casella, Alfredo	Pupazzetti	Ricordi
Chabrier, Emmanuel	Valse Romantique	International
Dvořák, Antonín	Waltzes	Boosey & Hawkes
Grieg, Edvard	Lyric Pieces	Various editions
Grieg, Edvard	Peer Gynt Suites	Schott
Ibert, Jacques	Histoires	Leduc, 1922
Krenek, Ernst	12 Short Piano Pieces	
Pachelbel, Johann	Variations	Ditson, 1914
Volkslieder	Klingende Heimat	Sikorski

(There are numerous collections of Baroque keyboard music.)

Muczynski, Robert	Maverick Pieces	G. Schirmer
Poulenc, Francis	Mouvements Perpetuels	Chester, 1939

Poulenc, Francis	Nocturnes	Heugel, 1932
Respighi, Ottorino	Antiche danze ed arie	Ricordi, 1919
Schubert, Franz	Lieder	Many editions
Turina, Joaquín	Jardin d'enfants	Salabert AMC
Turina, Joaquín	Ninerias	Salabert AMC

(The songs of Mozart, Reichardt, Beethoven, Schumann, Mendelssohn, Berlioz, Fauré, Hahn, and many others offer a wide variety of reading material.)

Bloch, Ernest	Visions et Propheties	G. Schirmer
Couperin, François	Ordres, 7 vols.	Various editions
Milhaud, Darius	Suadades do Brazil, 2 vols.	Eschig
Reger, Max	Aus Meinem Tagebuch, 4 vols.	AMP
Satie, Eric	Piano Music, 3 vols.	Salabert AMC
Scheidt, Samuel	Passamezzo Variations	Kalmus
Various composers	Fitzwilliam Virginal Book, 2 vols.	Dover

SCORES WITH DIFFICULT LEDGER-LINE PROBLEMS:

Britten, Benjamin	A Midsummer Night's Dream, vocal score pages 1, 203ff	Boosey & Hawkes
Britten, Benjamin	Albert Herring, vocal score pages 1ff	Boosey & Hawkes
Poulenc, Francis	Sextet for Piano and Winds, pages 13, 14, 18, 34	Hansen, 1945
Poulenc, Francis	Sonata for Cello & Piano, Fourth Movement	Heugel, 1953
Ravel, Maurice	Trio, Fourth Movement	Durand, 1915

SCORES WITH MULTIPLE VOICES:

Argento, Dominick	The Voyage of Edgar Allen Poe, vocal score pages 711 (8-part chorus); mixed ensemble pages 50–60, 200ff; TTBB, pages 394ff	Boosey & Hawkes
Bach, Johann Sebastian	Eleven Great Cantatas	Dover
Bach, Johann Sebastian	Six Great Secular Cantatas	Dover

Britten, Benjamin	Albert Herring, pages 72ff, 381ff	Boolsey & Hawkes
Britten, Benjamin	A Midsummer Night's Dream, pages 174ff, 242ff	Boosey & Hawkes

(The oratorios of Bach, Handel, and others provide hundreds of pages of choral scores for sightreading.)

Henze, Hans Werner	Elegie für junge Liebende, vocal score pages 437ff	Schott, 1961
Monteverdi, Claudio	Madrigals	Dover, 1986

(Numerous collections of motets and madrigals from the fifteenth, sixteenth, and seventeenth centuries provide splendid introductions to Renaissance styles.)

Bach, Johann Sebastian	Chorales, arranged in open score by Albert Riemenschneider	G. Schirmer
Puccini, Giacomo	*Turandot*, vocal score pages 94ff	Ricordi, 1944
Strauss, Richard	*Capriccio*, 2 great vocal octets, vocal score pages 182ff and 199ff	Boosey & Hawkes

REPRINTS OF FULL SCORES IN THE DOVER EDITIONS (A SERIES OF REPRINTS THAT IS ADDED TO EVERY YEAR):

Beethoven, Ludwig van	Symphonies I–VII	1976
Handel, Georg Friedrich	Complete Concerti Grossi	1981
Haydn, Joseph	London Symphonies, 2 vols.	1982
Haydn, Joseph	Symphonies 88–92	1982
Mendelssohn, Felix	Major Orchestral Works	No date
Mozart, Wolfgang Amadeus	17 Divertimenti	1979
Schubert, Franz	Four Symphonies	No date
Haydn, Joseph	String Quartets, 2 vols.	1980, 1982
Mozart, Wolfgang Amadeus	String Quartets	1970
Mozart, Wolfgang Amadeus	String Quintets	1978

ONE ORCHESTRAL REDUCTION THAT IS TOTALLY IMPOSSIBLE TO PLAY:

Henze, Hans Werner	Elegie für junge Liebende, vocal score pages 381–405	Boosey & Hawkes

MUSIC WITH COMPLEX RHYTHMIC PROBLEMS:

Bartók, Béla	Sonata	Boosey & Hawkes
Bartók, Béla	Out of Doors	Boosey & Hawkes
Bedford, David	Piano Pieces I and II (spatial notation)	Universal
Beethoven, Ludwig van	Sonata, Opus 111, Second Movement (mixed subdivision)	Many editions
Beethoven, Ludwig van	Sonata, Opus 109, Third Movement (mixed subdivision)	Many editions
Bernstein, Leonard	Sonata for Clarinet and Piano	Witmark, 1953
Boutry, Roger	En Images, 2 vols.	Salabert AMC
Britten, Benjamin	*Albert Herring* (mixed meter, pages 1ff)	Boosey & Hawkes
Britten, Benjamin	*Curlew River*	Faber, 1964
Britten, Benjamin	*The Burning Fiery Furnace*	Faber, 1966
Britten, Benjamin	*The Prodigal Son*	Faber, 1972

(In these three operas Britten employs rhythmic counterpoint, barless sections, and extensive mixed meter.)

Canteloube, Joseph	Danses Bretonnes	Salabert AMC
Castérède, Jacques	Diagrammes	Salabert AMC
Chávez, Carlos	Numerous Works for Piano	Mills
Copland, Aaron	Sonáta	Boosey & Hawkes
Corigliano, John	Etude Fantasy	G. Schirmer, 1981
Crumb, George	Five Piano Pieces	C. F. Peters
Crumb, George	Makrokosmos, 3 vols. (spatial notation, new forms)	C. F. Peters
Debussy, Claude	Etudes	Durand, 1914
Diamond, David	Eight Piano Pieces	G. Schirmer
Dohnányi, Ernst von	Sonata for Cello and Piano, pages 11ff, 22ff	International
Dutilleux, Henri	Sonata for Oboe & Piano, Third Movement	Leduc, 1947
Ginastera, Alberto	Numerous Works for Piano	Barry

Holst, Gustav	*Sāvitri* (mixed meter)	Faber, 1973	**83** *Suggested Music for* *Further Study*
Martin, Frank	Trio (rhythmic counterpoint)	Hug	
Messiaen, Olivier	Sept Visions de l'Amen	Durand, 1943	
Milhaud, Darius	Le Boeuf sur le Toit (rhythmic counterpoint)	G. Schirmer, 1981	
Orff, Carl	*Carmina Burana*	Schott	
Orff, Carl	*Catulli Carmina* (mixed meter)	Schott	
Ravel, Maurice	Trio, First and Second Movements	Durand, 1915	
Villa-Lobos, Heitor	Trio # 3, pages 6ff, 13, 48ff	Schott, 1929	

WORKS BY PAUL HINDEMITH THAT ABOUND IN RHYTHMIC COMPLEXITIES:

Sonata for Bass and Piano, pages 3–4, 14–16	Schott, 1950
Concerto for Trumpet and Bassoon, pages 1, 6, 35ff	Schott, 1949
Sonatas for Horn and Piano, pages 11, 12, 24, 30, 22, 24	Schott, 1939
Sonata for Oboe and Piano, pages 1–3, 16, 18	Schott, 1939
Sonata for Viola and Piano, page 5	Schott, 1922

SOME EXCELLENT RHYTHMIC PUZZLES, INCLUDING SEVERAL BARLESS SECTIONS, FROM THE WORKS OF CHARLES IVES:

Second Sonata, "Concord 1840–1860"	Arrow/AMP
From "Lincoln, the Great Commoner"	Peer, 1952
From "The Swimmers"	Merion, 1933
Immortality	Merion, 1933
Old Home Day	Peer, 1958
Premonitions	Merion, 1933
Two Little Flowers (7/8 against 4/4)	Merion, 1935

A TWENTIETH-CENTURY MILESTONE THAT SHOULD BE STUDIED:

Schoenberg, Arnold	*Pierrot Lunaire*	Universal (Belmont), 1914

COLLECTIONS OF PIANO DUETS:

Beethoven, Ludwig van	Variations	International
Benjamin, Arthur	Jamaican Rhumba	Boosey & Hawkes
Brahms, Johannes	Waltzes	Many editions
Dvořák, Antonín	Slavonic Dances	Boosey & Hawkes
Fauré, Gabriel	Dolly	International
Hindemith, Paul	Sonata	Schott
Messiaen, Olivier	Sept Visions de l'Amen	Durand, 1943
Milhaud, Darius	Enfantines	Eschig
Milhaud, Darius	Scaramouche	Eschig
Milhaud, Darius	Le Boeuf sur le toit	Eschig
Mozart, Wolfgang Amadeus	Leichte Sonatinen	C. F. Peters, 1939
Persichetti, Vincent	Serenade #8	Elkan-Vogel, 1956
Ravel, Maurice	Ma Mère l'oye	Durand, 1910
Satie, Erik	Aperçus desagreables	Eschig
Schubert, Franz	Selected Piano Works for 4 Hands	Dover, 1977

WORKS ARRANGED FOR TWO PIANOS, EIGHT HANDS:

Auber, Daniel-François-Esprit	Overture to *La Muette de Portici*	Simrock
Balakirev, Mily	Thamar	Breitkopf & Härtel
Beethoven, Ludwig van	Chorfantasie	Breitkopf & Härtel
Beethoven, Ludwig van	March from "Die Ruinen von Athen"	Breitkopf & Härtel
Beethoven, Ludwig van	March from *Egmont*	Breitkopf & Härtel
Beethoven, Ludwig van	Overture to *Fidelio*	Breitkopf & Härtel
Beethoven, Ludwig van	Overture "Leonore"	Breitkopf & Härtel
Beethoven, Ludwig van	Overture "Namens-feier"	Breitkopf & Härtel
Beethoven, Ludwig van	Overture "Egmont"	Breitkopf & Härtel
Beethoven, Ludwig van	Symphonies 1–9	Breitkopf & Härtel, Simrock
Bizet, Georges	Scherzo da Roma	Steingräber
Boieldieu, François-Adrien	Overture to "La dame blanche"	Simrock

Brahms, Johannes	Symphonies 1–4	Simrock
Brahms, Johannes	Overture "Akademisches Fest"	Simrock
Brahms, Johannes	Piano Concerto No. 2	Simrock
Brahms, Johannes	Serenades 1 and 2	Simrock
Brahms, Johannes	Sextets 1 and 2	Simrock
Brahms, Johannes	Tragische Overtüre	Simrock
Brahms, Johannes	2 Chorale Preludes, arr. Ohley-Watts	Schroeder & Gunther
Brahms, Johannes	Ungarische Tänze	Simrock, 1931
Brahms, Johannes	Variations on a Theme of Haydn	Simrock
Cherubini, Luigi	Overture to "Anacreon"	Simrock
Cherubini, Luigi	Overture to "Die Wasserträger"	Simrock
Chopin, Frédéric	Funeral March	Breitkopf & Härtel
Dvořák, Antonín	Legenden	Simrock
Dvořák, Antonín	Slavonische Tänze	Simrock
Dvořák, Antonín	Symphony No. 5	Simrock
Gade, Niels	*Ossian* Overture	Breitkopf & Härtel
Gluck, Christoph Willibald	Overture to *Alceste*	Simrock
Gluck, Christoph Willibald	Overture to *Iphegenia in Aulis*	Simrock
Grainger, Percy	Country Gardens	G. Schirmer
Handel, Georg Friedrich	3 Pieces from The Water Music, arranged by Carper	G. Schirmer
Liszt, Franz	Les Preludes	Breitkopf & Härtel
Lortzing, Albert	Overture to Zar und Zimmermann	Breitkopf & Härtel
Lortzing, Albert	Overture to Der Wildschütz	Breitkopf & Härtel
Méhul, Etienne-Nicolas	Overture "La Chasse du jeune Henri"	Simrock
Mendelssohn, Felix	Wedding March from "Sommernachtstraum"	Breitkopf & Härtel
Mendelssohn, Felix	Wedding March and Nocturne	Steingräber
Mendelssohn, Felix	War March from "Athalia"	Breitkopf & Härtel
Mendelssohn, Felix	Octet	Breitkopf & Härtel
Mendelssohn, Felix	Overture "Die schöne Melusine"	Simrock, Breitkopf & Härtel
Mendelssohn, Felix	Overture "Hebrides"	Simrock, Breitkopf & Härtel
Mendelssohn, Felix	Overture "Heimkehr aus der Ferne"	Breitkopf & Härtel

Mendelssohn, Felix	Overture "Meeresstille und glückliche Fahrt"	Simrock, Breitkopf & Härtel
Mendelssohn, Felix	Overture "Ruy Blas"	Breitkopf & Härtel
Mendelssohn, Felix	Overture to "Athalia"	Simrock, Breitkopf & Härtel
Mendelssohn, Felix	Overture, "Die Hochzeit des Camacho"	Breitkopf & Härtel
Mendelssohn, Felix	Overture to "Paulus"	Breitkopf & Härtel
Mendelssohn, Felix	Overture to "Sommer-nachtstraum"	Simrock
Mendelssohn, Felix	Trompeten-Overtüre	Breitkopf & Härtel
Mendelssohn, Felix	Symphonies 3 and 4	Breitkopf & Härtel
Meyerbeer, Giacomo	Coronation March from *Le Prophète*	Breitkopf & Härtel
Meyerbeer, Giacomo	Overture to *Les Huguenots*	Breitkopf & Härtel
Mozart, Wolfgang Amadeus	Overture to *Die Zauberflöte*	Simrock
Mozart, Wolfgang Amadeus	Overture to *Don Giovanni*	Simrock
Mozart, Wolfgang Amadeus	Overture to *Le nozze di Figaro*	Simrock
Reissiger, Karl Gottlieb	Overture to *Die Felsenmühle-zu Etalières*	Simrock
Rossini, Gioachino	Overture to *Il barbiere di Siviglia*	Simrock
Rossini, Gioachino	Overture to *Guilliaume Tell*	Steingräber
Rossini, Gioachino	Overture to *La gazza ladra*	Simrock
Rossini, Gioachino	Overture to *Tancredi*	Simrock
Rossini, Gioachino	Overture to *The Siege of Corinth*	Simrock
Rubinstein, Anton	Trot de Cavalerie	Steingräber
Schubert, Franz	Kindermarsch	Steingräber
Schubert, Franz	Marches, Opus 121, 40, 51	Steingräber
Schubert, Franz	Symphony in C Major	Breitkopf & Härtel
Schumann, Robert	Andante and Variations	Breitkopf & Härtel
Schumann, Robert	Quintet	Breitkopf & Härtel
Schumann, Robert	Symphonies 1 and 2	Breitkopf & Härtel
Schumann, Robert	Symphony No. 3	Simrock
Svendsen, Johan	Octet	Breitkopf & Härtel
Wagner, Richard	Faust Overture	Breitkopf & Härtel
Wagner, Richard	Three Selections from *Lohengrin*	Breitkopf & Härtel

Wagner, Richard	Prelude to *Tristan und Isolde*	Breitkopf & Härtel	
Weber, Carl Maria von	Overture *Jubel-Overture*	Simrock	
Weber, Carl Maria von	Overture to *Der Freischütz*	Simrock	
Weber, Carl Maria von	Overture to *Euryanthe*	Simrock	
Weber, Carl Maria von	Overture to *Oberon*	Simrock	
Weber, Carl Maria von	Overture to *Preciosa*	Simrock	

MUSICAL EXAMPLES

Example 1. Robert Schumann, *Album für die Jugend,* Opus 68, No. 1:
"Melodie"

Example 2. Robert Schumann, *Album für die Jugend,* Opus 68, No. 3: "Trällerliedchen"

Example 3. Robert Schumann, *Album für die Jugend*, Opus 68, No. 6: "**Armes Waisenkind**"

Example 4. Robert Schumann, *Album für die Jugend,* Opus 68, No. 5: **"Stückchen"**

Example 5. Johann Sebastian Bach, *Notenbüchlein für Anna Magdalena Bach,* **Menuet**

Example 6. Johann Sebastian Bach, *Notenbüchlein für Anna Magdalena Bach,* **Polonaise**

Example 7. Johann Sebastian Bach, *Notenbüchlein für Anna Magdalena Bach*, **Marche**

Example 8. Johann Sebastian Bach, **Little Prelude in D Minor,** BWV 926

Little Prelude in D Minor

Example 9. Robert Schumann, *Album für die Jugend,* Opus 68, No. 14: "Kleine Studie"

Example 10. Robert Schumann, *Album für die Jugend,* Opus 68, No. 35: "**Mignon**"

Example 11. Béla Bartók, *For Children,* Volume 3, No. 13: "**Anička Mlynárova**"

Example 12. Béla Bartók, *For Children*, Volume 3, No. 14:
"Plowing Are Six Oxen"

Example 13. Johann Sebastian Bach, **Little Prelude in E Minor,**
BWV 941

Example 14. Béla Bartók, *For Children*, Volume 3, No. 5:
"The Peacock Flew," measures 1–40

Example 15. Johann Sebastian Bach, **Fughetta in C Minor**, BWV 961

Fughetta in C Minor

Example 17. Béla Bartók, *For Children*, Volume 4, No. 42:
"Mourning Song"

Example 18. Frédéric Chopin, **Prelude in B Minor**, Opus 28, No. 6

Example 19. Felix Mendelssohn, *Songs Without Words,* Opus 19, No. 2: **"Regrets"**

Example 20. Robert Schumann, *Albumblätter*, Opus 124, No. 4: "**Waltz**"

Example 21. Robert Schumann, *Albumblätter*, Opus 124, No. 6: "Little Lullaby"

Example 22. Alexander Scriabin, **Prelude in E Major**, Opus 11, No. 9

Example 23. Alexander Scriabin, **Prelude in C-Sharp Minor**, Opus 11, No. 10

Example 24. Franz Schubert, **Children's March in G Major,** D. 928

Example 25. Franz Schubert, **Four Ländler,** D. 814

Secondo.

Primo.

Four Ländler

Secondo.

Primo.

Examples 26a and 26b. Johann Froberger, **Two Sarabandes**

Examples 27a–d. Johann Kirnberger, Four Small Pieces:
Polonaise, Menuet, La Lutine, La Gaillarde

Polonaise, Menuet, La
Lutine, La Gaillarde

Examples 28a, b. Friedrich Marpurg, Two Small Pieces:
Menuet, La Badine

Menuet, La Badine

Examples 29a, b. Christoph Nichelmann, Two Small Pieces:
La Gaillarde, La Tendre

Example 30. Edward MacDowell, *Sea Pieces:* "**Starlight**"

The stars are but the cherubs
That sing about the throne
Of gray old Ocean's spouse,
Fair Moon's pale majesty.

Example 31. William Schuman, *Three-Score Set:* **II**

Example 32. Edvard Grieg, *Lyric Pieces,* Opus 57, No. 6: **"Hjemve,"** measures 28–56

From Edition Peters 3100a
Used by permission of C. F. Peters Corporation

133

"Hjemve"

Example 33. Edvard Grieg, *Lyric Pieces,* Opus 71, No. 2: "Sommeraften"

"Sommeraften"

Example 34. Ernest Bloch, *Poems of the Sea:* **"Chanty"**

Example 35. Johann Sebastian Bach, Partita in A Minor, BWV 827:
Allemande, measures 1–6

1) $\frac{1}{16}$ instead of $\frac{1}{32}$ in 'G'. 2) (G). 3) Middle voice in 'G': 4) The ~ appears in 'G'.

5) in 'G'. 6) The succession *c sharp d sharp* instead of *c d*, (G). 7) (G).

Example 36. Johann Sebastian Bach, **Sonata in G Major for Viola da Gamba and Cembalo,** BWV 1027: *Adagio,* measures 1–8

Sonata in G Major for
Viola da Gamba and
Cembalo

Example 37. Benjamin Britten, *The Turn of the Screw,* tone-row

Example 38. Alban Berg, *Lulu,* tone-row

Example 39. Alban Berg, **Concerto for Violin and Orchestra,** tone-row

Example 40. Arnold Schoenberg, **Five Piano Pieces,** Opus 23, tone-row

Example 41. Dan Welcher, **Dance Variations,** tone-row

Example 42. Stephen Foster, "Old Folks at Home"

Words and Music by E. P. CHRISTY.

Way down upon de Swanee ribber, Far, far a--way,

Dere's wha my heart is turning ebber, Dere's wha de old folks stay.

Example 43. Stephen Foster, "**Beautiful Dreamer**"

Example 44. Anonymous, "The Nightingale"

Ad libitum, at good narration speed

1. One morn-ing, one morn-ing, one morn-ing in May, I met a fair
2. Good morn-ing, good morn-ing, good morn-ing to thee; And where are you
3. They had-n't been stand-ing but one hour or two, When out of his

cou-ple a-mak-ing their way. And one was a la-dy so___
go-ing my pret-ty la-dy? O, I am a-go-ing to the
knap-sack a fid-dle he drew. The tunes that he play'd made the___

neat and so fair, The_ oth-er a sol-dier, a ___ brave vol-un-teer.
banks of the sea, To see the wa-ters a-glid-ing, hear the night-in-gale sing.
val-leys to ring, O see the wa-ters a-glid-ing, hear the night-in-gale sing!

4. "Pretty lady, pretty lady,
    it's time to give o'er."
"O no, pretty soldier,
    please play one tune more;
I'd rather hear your fiddle,
    or the touch of one string,
Than see the waters a-gliding,
    hear the nightingale sing."

5. "Pretty soldier, pretty soldier,
    will you marry me?"
"O no, pretty lady,
    that never can be,
For I have a wife in London
    and children twice three.
Two wives in the Army
    is too many for me."

Example 45. Anonymous, "Barb'ry Allan"

Barb'ry Allan

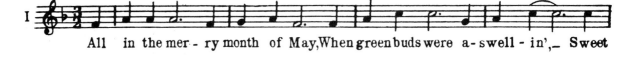

All in the mer-ry month of May, When green buds were a-swell-in',_ Sweet

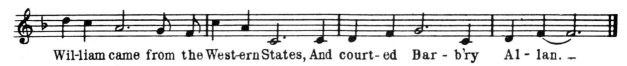

Wil-liam came from the West-ern States, And court-ed Bar-b'ry Al-lan. _

Example 46. Stephen Foster, "Come Where My Love Lies Dreaming"

*"Come Where My Love
Lies Dreaming"*

152

"Come Where My Love
Lies Dreaming"

Grave par Lawson.

Example 47. Claudio Monteverdi, "Cor mio"

"Cor mio"

1) **Nell'originale:**

e per te na to mo — re.

Example 48. Claudio Monteverdi, **"Cruda Amarilli,"** measures 1–35

Example 49. Giuseppe Verdi, *Aïda:* Act II, Scene 2, measures 475–487

Example 50. Anonymous, "The Riddle Song"

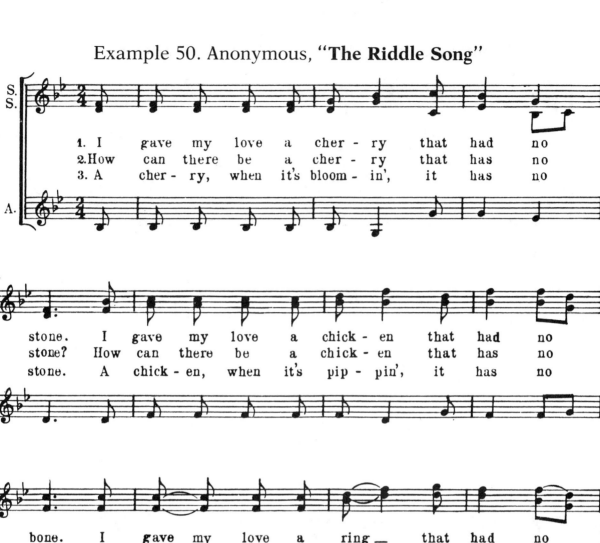

1. I gave my love a cher - ry that had no
2. How can there be a cher - ry that has no
3. A cher - ry, when it's bloom - in', it has no

stone. I gave my love a chick - en that had no
stone? How can there be a chick - en that has no
stone. A chick - en, when it's pip - pin', it has no

bone. I gave my love a ring ___ that had no
bone? How can there be a ring ___ that has no
bone. A ring, ___ when it's rol - lin', it has no

end. I gave my love a ba - by with no cry - en.
end? How can there be a ba - by with no cry - en?
end. A ba - by, when it's sleep - in', has no cry - en.

Example 51. Anonymous, "The Inconstant Lover"

S. S.

1. O, Jack - ie's on the wa - ter, let him sink or let him
2. O, meet - ing is a pleas - ure and — part - ing is —
3. The grave will de - cay you, and — turn you to —
4. For - sak - en, for - sak - en, for - sak - en am —

A.

swim; For if he can live with - out me I can live with - out
grief; But an in - con - stant true - love is — worse than a
dust; Is there one man out of twen - ty a — poor girl can
I. But he's cer - tain - ly mis - tak - en if he thinks that I'll

him! O, Jack - ie is a young boy but still young - er am
thief. A thief will but — rob you and — take all you
trust? They'll hug you and — kiss you and — make your heart
cry! I'll take off this — black dress and — flour - ish in

I; And how of - ten has he told me that he'd wed me or die.
have, But an in - con - stant true - love will take you to your grave.
warm, But as soon as your back's turned They'll laugh you to scorn.
green, I don't care if I'm for - sak - en for I'm on - ly six - teen.

Example 52. Anonymous, "The Mingo Mountains"

Example 53. Anonymous, "Go Bury Me Beneath the Willow"

1. Go bur - y me be - neath the wil - low, Be-
2. To - mor - row was our wed - ding day but __
3. They told me that she did not love me, __
4. Plant on my grave a snow - white lil - y, That

neath the weep - ing wil - low tree, And when she knows that
now, O God, the wear - y keep; She's gone, she's gone to
But I could not think it true; Un - til an an - gel
she may know my love was true; And tell her that I

I am sleep - ing, Then per - haps she'll think of me.
love some oth - er, She no long - er cares for me.
soft - ly whis - p'red, "She has prov - en false to you."
died to save her Though my heart she nev - er knew.

Example 54. Georg Friedrich Handel, *Neun deutsche Arien:* No. 1, "Künft'ger Zeiten"

"Künft'ger Zeiten"

Example 55. Johann Sebastian Bach, Cantata *Gott, der Herr, ist Sonn' und Schild* (BWV 79): Aria, **"Gott ist unser Sonn' und Schild!"**

*"Gott ist unser Sonn' und
Schild!"*

Gott ist un_ser Sonn'und Schild!

Gott ist un_ser Sonn'und Schild, Gott ist un_ser

Sonn' und Schild, Gott ist un_ser Sonn' und Schild,_____ un_ser Sonn' und

Schild,_____ un_ser Sonn_____ und Schild,_____ Sonn und Schild!

Dal Segno.

Example 56. Johann Sebastian Bach, Cantata *Gott, der Herr, ist Sonn'* und Schild (BWV 79): Chorale, **"Nun danket Alle Gott"**

"Nun danket Alle Gott"

Example 57. Johann Sebastian Bach, Cantata *Gott, der Herr, ist Sonn'* und Schild (BWV 79): Chorale, **"Erhalt' uns in der Wahrheit"**

Example 58. Johann Sebastian Bach, Cantata *O Ewigkeit, du Donnerwort* (BWV 60): Chorale, **"Es ist genug"**

Example 59. Johann Sebastian Bach, Cantata *Sie werden aus Saba Alle kommen* (BWV 65): Chorale, **"Ei nun, mein Gott"**

Example 60. Wolfgang Amadeus Mozart, **Divertimento**, K. 113: *Allegro*, measures 1–53

Divertimento

Example 61. Wolfgang Amadeus Mozart, **Divertimento**, K. 131: **Menuet**

Menuet

Menuetto da c.

Menuetto da capo.

Example 62. Wolfgang Amadeus Mozart, Divertimento, K. 186:
Allegro assai; **Menuet**

Menuetto da capo.

Example 63. Ludwig van Beethoven, **Symphony No. 7 in A Major**, Opus 92: I: *Poco sostenuto; vivace*, measures 63–94

Symphony No. 7 in A
Major

Example 64a. Felix Mendelssohn, *Ein Sommernachtstraum:*
III. Song with Chorus, measures 1–8

Example 64b. Felix Mendelssohn, *Ein Sommernachtstraum*:
III. Song with Chorus, measures 44–59

Example 65. Richard Wagner, *Lohengrin:* Act III, measures 1–48

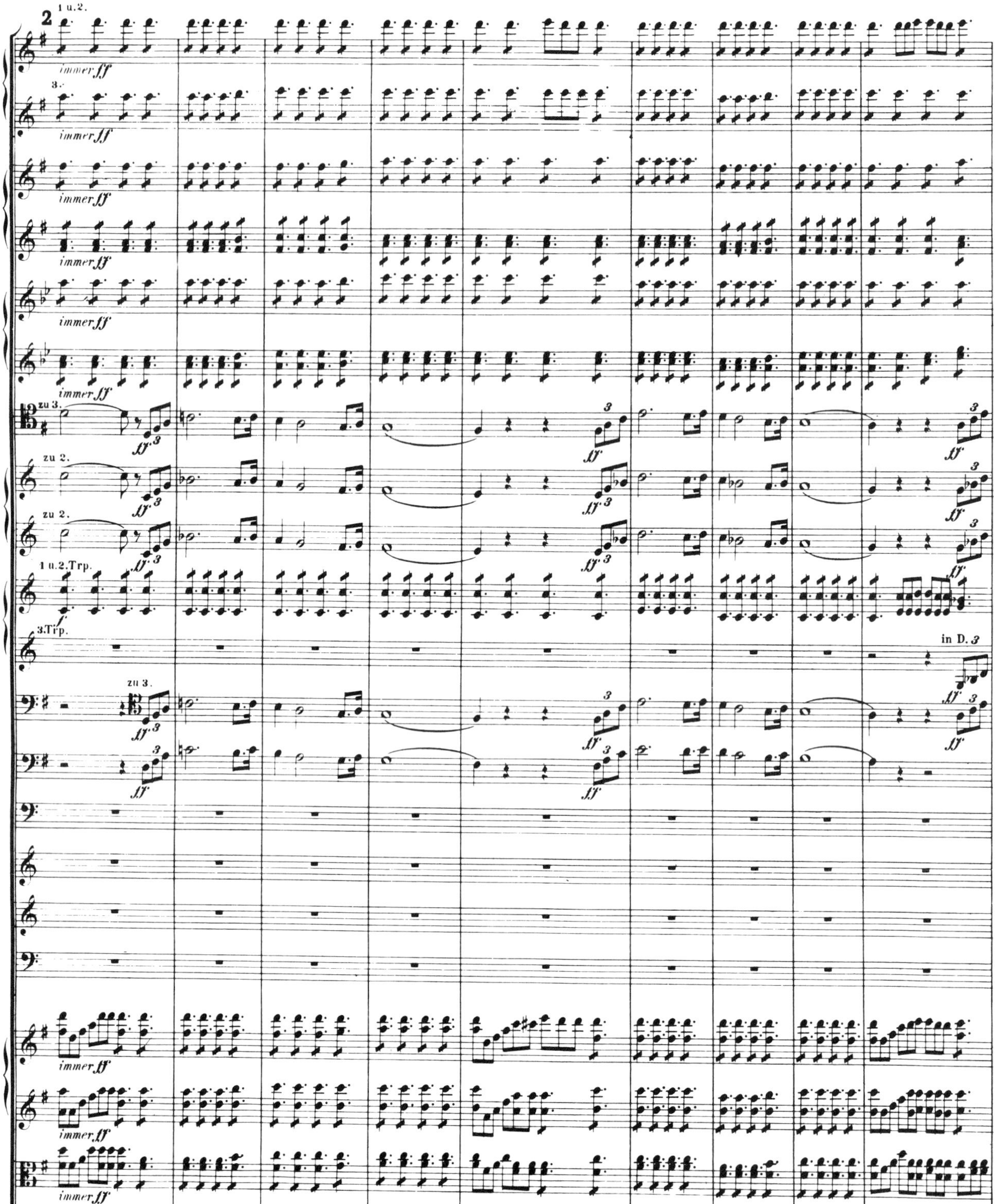
2
1 u.2.
3.
immer ff
zu 3.
zu 2.
1 u.2.Trp.
3.Trp.
in D.
2

Example 66. Franz Joseph Haydn, Quartet in B-flat Major, Opus 64, No. 2: **Menuetto**

III

M. D. C.

Example 67. Wolfgang Amadeus Mozart, **Quartet in G Major**, K. 156:
Presto

Quartet in G Major

Example 68. Wolfgang Amadeus Mozart, **Quintet in B-flat Major,**
K. 174: *Menuetto ma allegretto*

Trio.

Example 69. Robert Schumann, **"So lasst mich scheinen,"**
Opus 98a, No. 9: measures 1–19

Example 70. Robert Schumann, "**Zigeunerliedchen**," Opus 79, No. 8

Example 71. Edward MacDowell, **Second Concerto for Piano and** Orchestra in D Minor, Opus 23: III, measures 126–144

Example 72. Christoph Willibald von Gluck, *Orfeo ed Euridice:* "Che puro ciel"

208

ORPHEUS.

How pure a light!
Che pu - ro ciel!
the sun is
che chia - ro

clear!
sol!
So bright
che nuo - - va
his
va

Example 73. Gustav Mahler, "Liebst du um Schönheit"

Liebst du um Schönheit, o nicht mich liebe!	*If you love for beauty, oh do not love me!*
Liebe die Sonne, sie trägt ein gold'nes Haar!	*Love the sun, adorned by golden hair!*
Liebst du um Jugend, o nicht mich liebe!	*If you love for youth, oh do not love me!*
Liebe den Frühling, der jung ist jedes Jahr!	*Love the spring, it is young every year!*
Liebst du um Schätze, o nicht mich liebe!	*If you love for treasures, oh do not love me!*
Liebe die Meerfrau, sie hat viel Perlen klar!	*Love the mermaid, she has many shimmering pearls!*
Liebst du um Liebe, o ja, mich liebe!	*If you love for love, oh yes, then love me!*
Liebe mich immer, dich lieb' ich immer, immerdar!	*Love me always, I love you forever, forever!*

FRIEDRICH RUECKERT

English translations by EDITH BRAUN

Example 74. Gustav Holst, **Sāvitri,** measures 177–199

robe   Thou art en - shroud - ed in my

love.   With my song   I weave a spell.

cresc.

E - vil pow'rs   may not ap - proach   with-in the hear - ing of my

voice   On - ly the gods may en - ter   here _____ in

Example 75. Maurice Ravel, *Ma Mère l'Oye*: II. "**Petit Poucet**"

*Il croyait trouver aisément son chemin par le moyen de son pain qu'il avait semé
partout où il avait passé; mais il fut bien surpris lorsqu'il n'en put retrouver une
seule miette: les oiseaux étaient venus qui avaient tout mangé.* (Ch. Perrault.)

"Petit Poucet"

SECONDA

Example 76. Maurice Ravel, **L'Enfant et les Sortilèges**, measures 1–40

Une pièce à la campagne (plafond très bas), donnant sur un jardin. Une maison normande, ancienne, ou mieux: démodée; de grands fauteuils, houssés; une haute horloge en bois à cadran fleuri. Une tenture à petits personnages, bergerie. Une cage ronde à écureuil, pendue près de la fenêtre. Grande cheminée à hotte, un reste de feu paisible, une bouilloire qui ronronne. Le Chat aussi. C'est l'après-midi.

The scene presents a room in the country (ceiling very low) opening on a garden. A Normandy house, old, or rather, old-fashioned; large arm-chairs covered with cloth, a tall wooden clock with a decorated dial. Wallpaper depicting pastoral scenes. A round cage with a squirrel in it, hanging near the window. A large fireplace where a small fire burns peacefully. A teakettle purrs, the cat also. It is afternoon.

The Child, six or seven years old, is seated before a task which he has just begun. He is extremely lazy. He bites his penholder, scratches his head and sings softly.

L'Enfant, six ou sept ans, est assis devant un devoir commencé. Il est en pleine crise de paresse, il mord son porte-plume, se gratte la tête et chantonne à demi-voix.

THE CHILD
L'ENFANT

J'ai pas envie de faire ma pa _ ge,
I do not want to learn my les _ son,

J'ai en _ vie d'al _ ler me   promener.
I'd much rath _ er   go   for a walk.

J'ai en _ vie de manger tous les gâ _
And I   wish   I might eat up all the

_ teaux.
cakes.

J'ai envie de ti _ rer la queue du chat Et de cou _
Oh, how I'd like to pull the cat's tail ver _ y hard And

l'En. -per cel le de l'E cureuil! J'ai envie de gronder tout le mon de! J'ai envie de met
cut off the squirrel's too! *I wish I might growl at every bod y.* *Oh, how I'd like to*

l'En. tre Maman en pé ni ten ce.
make Ma ma feel ver y sor ry.

The door opens. Enter Mama (or rather as much as can be seen with the ceiling very low and the entire scale of all the furnishings and all the objects in exaggerated dimensions in order to make more striking the smallness of the Child) that is to say a skirt, the lower part of a silk apron, a steel chain from which hangs a pair of scissors, and a hand. This hand is raised with the index finger pointing.

La porte s'ouvre. Entre Maman (ou plûtot ce qu'en laissent voir de plafond très bas et l'échelle de tout le décor où tous les objets assument des dimensions exagérées, pour rendre frappante la petitesse de l'Enfant) c'est-à-dire une jupe, le bas d'un tablier de soie, la chaîne d'acier où pend une paire de ciseaux, et une main. Cette main se lève, interroge de l'index.

MAMAN, affectueusement. *MAMA, affectionately.*

Bé bé a é té sage? Il a fi ni sa page?
My child have you been good? *And learned your les son well?*

Più animato. ♩ = 76

Rit.

Suivez

The Child makes no reply and pouting, slips down low in his chair. The skirt moves forward, one hand over the copybook. The other hand, higher, holds a tray on which are a teapot and a cup.

L'Enfant ne répond rien et se laisse glisser, boudeur, en bas de sa chaise. La robe s'avance sur la scène, une main tendue au-dessus du cahier. L'autre main, plus haute, soutient un plateau portant la théière et la tasse du goûter.

a Tempo Rit.

Ma. Oh, tu n'as rien fait! Tu as é claboussé d'encre le ta pis!
Oh, you have done noth ing! *You've carelessly spattered the carpet with ink!*

a Tempo Rit.

Example 77. Jacques Murgier, **Capriccio for Oboe and Piano**

*Capriccio for Oboe and
Piano*

Example 78. Verne Reynolds, Echo Variations for Oboe and Piano: III. "Crystals"

Example 79. Paul Hindemith, Sonata for Viola and Piano Opus 11, No. 4: II. **Theme and Variations,** measures 1–33

Example 80. Paul Hindemith, Sonata for Violoncello and Piano Opus 11, No. 3: II. **Thema mit Variationen,** measures 82–109

Example 81. Roy Harris, *Little Suite:* I. "Bells"

Piano

Example 82. Erik Satie, **Gnossienne,** No. 1

Très luisant (Shining)

Questionnez (Questionning)

Gnossienne, No. 1

Du bout de la pensée (From the tip of the thought)

Postulez en vous-même (Wonder about yourself)

Pas à Pas (Step by Step)

Sur la langue (On the tip of the tongue)

Example 83. Erik Satie, *Descriptions Automatiques:*
I. "Sur un Vaisseau"

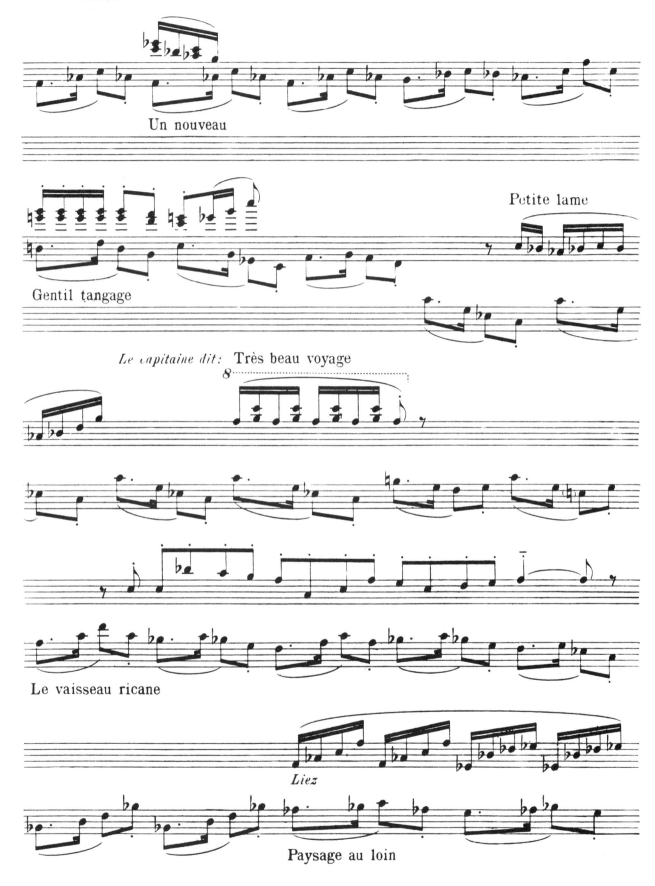

Un nouveau

Gentil tangage

Petite lame

Le capitaine dit: Très beau voyage

Le vaisseau ricane

Liez

Paysage au loin

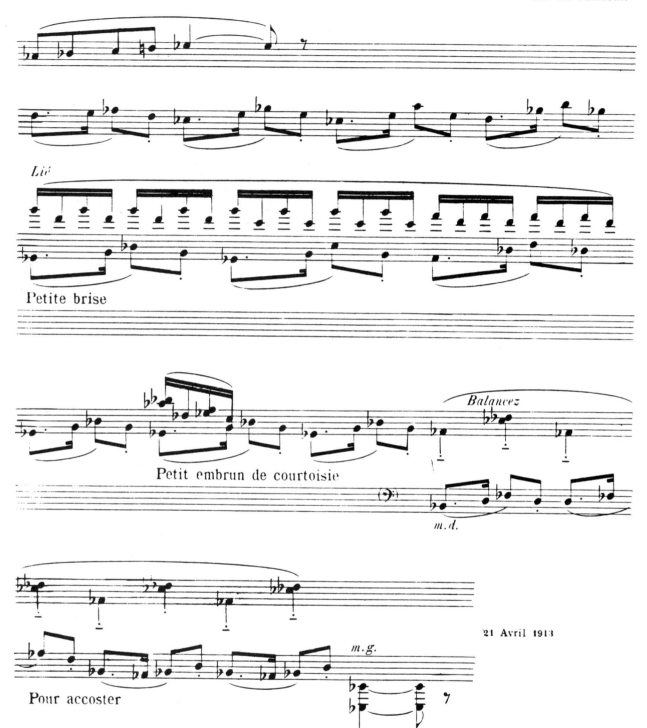

Lié

Petite brise

Petit embrun de courtoisie

Balancez

m.d.

21 Avril 1913

m.g.

Pour accoster

Example 84. Erik Satie, *Aiurs à faire fuir:* **III**

Dernièrement (Lastly)

Aiurs à faire fuir

Example 85a. Bohuslav Martinů, Trio: III. *Allegro,* measures 1–9

Example 85b. Bohuslav Martinů, Trio: III. *Allegro,* measures 21–31

Example 85c. Bohuslav Martinů, Trio, V. *Allegro con brio*, measures 50–80

Example 86. Giacomo Puccini, *Madama Butterfly*, Act I, measures 1–31

Example 87a. Dan Welcher, **Dance Variations:** Variation I, measures 9–30

Example 87b. Dan Welcher, **Dance Variations:** Variation VI, measures
28–34

Example 88a. Verne Reynolds, Quintet for Piano and Winds: I. **Toccata,** measures 1–7

247

Toccata

Example 88b. Verne Reynolds, Quintet for Piano and Winds: II.
Cantilena, measures 1–14

Example 88c. Verne Reynolds, Quintet for Piano and Winds:
III. *Allegro,* measures 36–46

Example 89a. Arnold Schoenberg: *Pierrot Lunaire,* "**Mondfleck,**" measures 13–16

Example 89b. Arnold Schoenberg: *Pierrot Lunaire,* "**Die Kreuze,**"
measures 5–9

Pierrot Lunaire

Example 90. Robert Schumann, **Allegro in B Minor**, Opus 8, measures 105–139

Allegro in B Minor

Example 91. Iannis Xenakis, **Herma,** measures 89–113

Herma

Example 92. Karlheinz Stockhausen, **Klavierstück IX,** measures 134–152

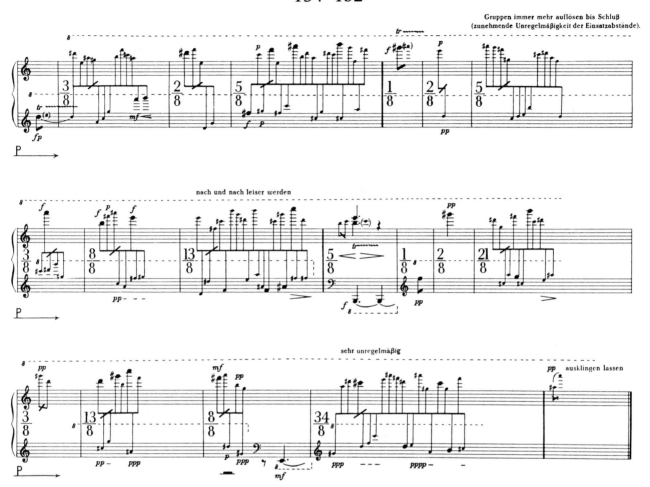

Example 93. David Bedford, **Piano Piece 2**, lines 1–5

Example 94. Morton Feldman, *Durations III* for Violin, Piano, and Tuba: **II**

Example 95. Earle Brown, **Music for Cello and Piano,** lines 1–3

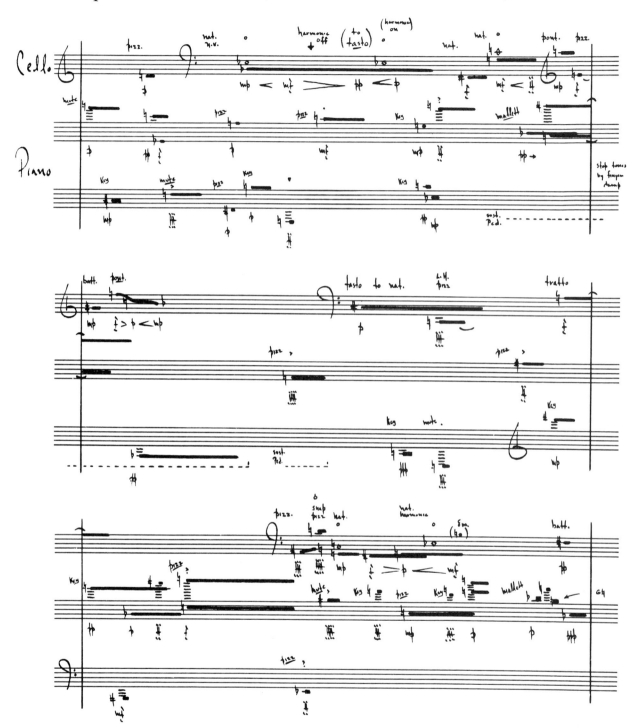

Example 96. Wolfgang Steffen, **Les Spirales,** Opus 36, lines 1–5

Example 97. William Albright, Five Chromatic Dances:
III. **Fantasy—Mazurka,** lines 1–3

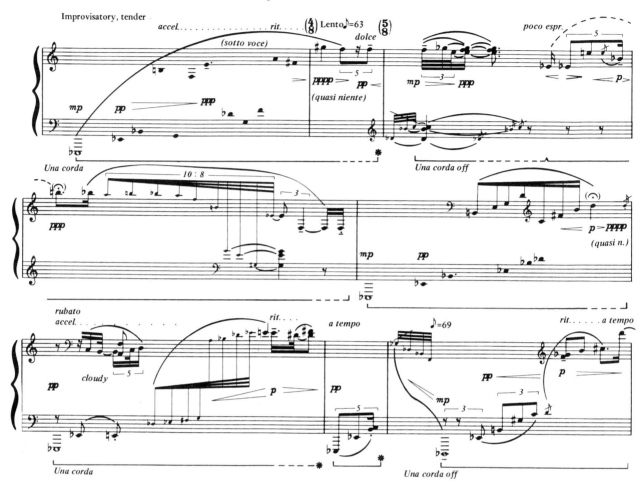

Example 98a. Kamran Ince, **Beyond Black,** lines 1–6

Example 98b. Kamran Ince, **Beyond Black**, lines 38–43

Bibliography

Bloom, Benjamin S., ed. *Developing Talent in Young People.* New York: Ballantine, 1985.

Chomsky, Noam. *Aspects of the Theory of Syntax.* Cambridge, Mass.: MIT Press, 1965.

Fiske, Roger. *Score Reading.* 4 vols. Oxford: Oxford University Press, 1955–1960.

Gordon, Edwin E. *Learning Sequences in Music.* Chicago: G.I.A. Publications, 1980.

Green, Barry, and W. Timothy Gallwey. *The Inner Game of Music.* Garden City, N.Y.: Anchor Press, 1986.

Grutzmacher, Patricia Ann. "The Effect of Tonal Pattern Training on the Aural Perception." *Journal of Research in Music Education* 35, no. 3 (1985): 171–181.

Hirsch, E. D., Jr. *Cultural Literacy.* Boston: Houghton Mifflin, 1987.

Jacob, Gordon. *How to Read a Score.* London: Hawkes, 1944.

Keilmann, Wilhelm. *Introduction to Sightreading at the Piano or Other Keyboard Instrument.* 2 vols. Translated by Kurt Michaelis. Frankfurt: C. F. Peters, 1970–1972.

Lloyd, Norman, and Ruth and Jan DeGaetani. *The Complete Sightsinger.* New York: Harper and Row, 1980.

Martin, Louis, and Robert Levin. *Sight Singing, Ear Training, and Literature.* New York: Prentice-Hall, 1988.

Melcher, Robert A., and Willard F. Warch. *Music for Score Reading.* Englewood Cliffs, N.J.: Prentice-Hall, 1971.

Neisser, Ulric. *Cognitive Psychology.* New York: Appleton-Century-Crofts, 1967.

Pembrook, Randall G. "The Effect of Vocalization on Melody Memory Conservation." *Journal of Research in Music Education* 35, no. 3 (1985): 155–169.

Ristad, Eloise. *A Soprano on Her Head.* Boulder, Colo.: Real People, 1982.

Rood, Louise. *An Introduction to the Orchestra Score.* New York: Kalmus, 1948.

Smith, Frank. *Understanding Reading.* New York: Holt, Rinehart, and Winston, 1971.

Street, Eric. "Bridging the Gap Between Sight Reading and Memorizing." *American Music Teacher* 37, no. 2 (1987): 32–33.

Taylor, Bob. *Sight-Reading Chord Progressions.* Los Angeles: J. Taylor, 1983.

———. *Sight-reading Jazz.* 2 vols. Los Angeles: J. Taylor, 1983.